MESSERSCHMITT
Bf109
1935 onwards (all marks)

First published in October 2009

A catalogue record for this book is available from the British
Library

ISBN 978 184425 6426

Library of Congress control no. 2009927968

Published by Haynes Publishing,
Sparkford, Yeovil, Somerset BA22 7JJ, UK
Tel: 01963 442030 Fax: 01963 440001
Int. tel: +44 1963 442030 Int. fax: +44 1963 440001
E-mail: sales@haynes.co.uk
Website: www.haynes.co.uk

Haynes North America Inc.,
861 Lawrence Drive, Newbury Park, California 91320, USA

Designed and typeset by James Robertson
Printed and bound in the UK

WARNING
While every attempt has been made throughout this book
to emphasise the safety aspects of working on, restoring
and flying a Messerschmitt Bf109, the authors and
publishers accept no liability whatsoever for any damage,
injury or loss resulting from the use of this book.

COVER CUTAWAY: Messerschmitt Bf109G/K
(courtesy Art Tech/Aerospace Publishing)

MESSERSCHMITT Bf109

1935 onwards (all marks)

Owners' Workshop Manual

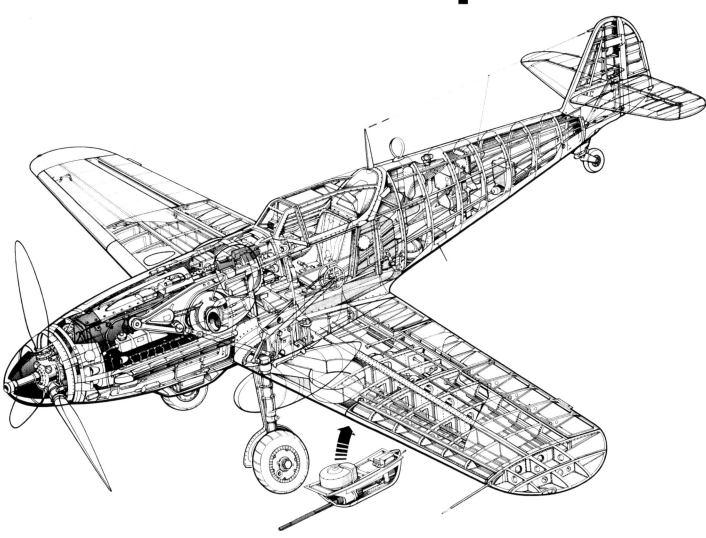

An insight into owning, flying and maintaining
the Luftwaffe's legendary single-seat fighter

Paul Blackah and Malcolm V. Lowe

Contents

OPPOSITE: A Luftwaffe pilot climbs down from his Messerschmitt Bf109E of Jagdgeschwader 53 'Pik-As' (Ace of Spades) in Northern France in 1940.
Arthur Grimm/Ullstein Bild/TopFoto

Acknowledgements

Several major personalities in the aircraft preservation and historical research world were of great help in the compiling of this book. In particular, a profound vote of thanks is made to Russ Snadden, not only for his assistance with material for this publication, but for his enthusiasm and determination over many years in the restoration to airworthy condition of Bf109G-2 Black 6, the aircraft on which we are focusing here. Similarly, great thanks are expressed to all the members of the Black 6 team for their assistance and support, not just with the Black 6 project, but for help with information and photographs.

Professionals in the aircraft restoration business were also of great assistance, particularly Steve Vizard, who is very much in the front line of the high standards of workmanship that are to be seen in several currently airworthy historic aircraft. In similar fashion, a number of pilots who have flown Black 6 also contributed to this project, including Charlie Brown, Cliff Spink and Dave Southwood. From an earlier generation, Eric 'Winkle' Brown, a Royal Navy test pilot who flew and evaluated captured Bf109s during the Second World War, also enthusiastically helped with research and reminiscences. A number of historians in Germany and Britain were of great assistance, including Pete Redhead, Jim Smith, Andy Sweet and Peter Walter, while John Batchelor, Philip Jarrett, Jaroslav Matoulek, Michal Ovčáčík, Tomáš Poruba and Graham Young all helped by providing rare archive photographs. Assistance was also provided by the Vojenský Historický Ústav in Prague, Czech Republic. Last, but by no means least, Louise Blackah and Victor Lowe worked with great enthusiasm behind the scenes on the preparation of this book and in the checking of text and proofs.

Thank you from the co-authors to all of these contributors.

Authors' note

Why the Bf109G-2 was chosen as the subject for this book

The G-2 version of the Bf109 series was chosen as the focus of this book for a number of reasons. First and foremost it is because the G-2 is the mark of 'Black 6', the well-known and authentic Bf109G-2 that flew for a number of years in Britain during the 1990s. This aircraft was a genuine German-built, Daimler-Benz DB605-powered, Luftwaffe-operated, combat veteran, and as such was a unique historic aircraft that always drew much interest and admiration from those who saw it performing in its natural element at air shows. This background is the opposite to other airworthy Bf109 lookalikes, which more often than not are post-Second World War, Spanish-built Hispano Buchóns, which either retain their Rolls-Royce Merlin engines, or have been re-engined by their owners with the DB605 engine – and thus made to look like German-built Bf109s.

Black 6 became a well-known and much-loved participant at air shows and commemorative events in Britain, and a great deal of the affection shown to this aircraft stemmed from it being a genuine, priceless and irreplaceable combat veteran from the Second World War. For that reason alone it is worthy of being the focus of this book, but it is also a well-documented aircraft for which a large amount of information and background material exists. This means that much of the documentation and detailed photography in this book can focus specifically on this very special aircraft, and its specific model number and engineering.

Black 6 was made airworthy at the end of a very long restoration period by a dedicated team of which Flight Lieutenant Russ Snadden was at the head. Without official funding and faced on occasion with official indifference, these dedicated restorers nevertheless achieved their ultimate goal of returning Black 6 to the air from the perilous state into which it had been allowed to deteriorate. The story of that restoration on the following pages is a testament to the devoted work that they performed on Black 6, as well as their sheer determination to ensure that Black 6 was restored to the highest standards. There is another good reason why Black 6 is the subject matter of much of what is to be found on the following pages – one of the co-authors, Paul Blackah, worked on Black 6, thus putting him in a unique position to describe many of the technical aspects of this very genuine and priceless aircraft.

OPPOSITE: 'Black 6' – Messerschmitt Bf109G2, Werk Nummer 10639 – was the first genuine Second World War German fighter aircraft to fly again. She is pictured over the Cambridgeshire countryside following her nineteen-year restoration.
Richard Paver

Introduction

The iconic Messerschmitt Bf109 was one of the most famous warplanes of the Second World War era, and is arguably among the greatest combat aircraft of all time. It was one of Germany's principal fighter aircraft during the war, and was a worthy and often deadly opponent to Allied planes. It was a contemporary of the legendary Supermarine Spitfire, and like the Spitfire was one of the few high-performance front-line aircraft of its time to be produced and to fight throughout the war, from start to finish.

LEFT: Now flying in North America and civil-registered as CF-EML, this completely rebuilt and restored Bf109E-4 was the result of many years of painstaking work, much of it carried out in Britain by experts including Airframe Assemblies. The aircraft was originally built as a Bf109E-1, Werk Nummer 3579, but was brought up to E-4 standard and possibly later to E-7, and is painted in the markings that it wore during the Battle of Britain in 1940 when assigned to I. (Jagd)/Lehrgeschwader 2. In fact 'White 14' is believed to have been flown by the legendary Luftwaffe fighter ace Hans-Joachim Marseille at that time. It is currently owned by the Russell Aviation Group in Canada. *Jerry Day*

Destined from the start to become one of
history's great fighter aircraft, the Bf109
proved to be a major success from the start of
its operational service in 1937, and was flown
by the highest-scoring fighter pilots the world
has ever seen. It made a major impact over
Spain in its first conflict from 1937 onwards,
and later played a key role for Germany in the
Second World War. Indeed, it was in operation
throughout that combat, one of only a few
warplanes that could claim that honour.

Built in large numbers in many different
versions, the origins of this fine aircraft go back
to the years immediately after the Nazi takeover
in Germany. The Bayerische Flugzeugwerke
AG (later, from 1938, the Messerschmitt AG)
began design work on an exceptional all-metal
fighter which drew on some aspects of the
advanced Bf108 light touring aircraft. With
considerable design input from the talented
Willy Messerschmitt himself, the new aircraft
emerged as a clean, streamlined cantilever
low-wing monoplane with a retractable

undercarriage. The tailplane was braced on early
models, this bracing later being dispensed with.
The aircraft was initially intended to be powered
by the Junkers Jumo inline piston engine, but
the prototype was powered by a Rolls-Royce
Kestrel engine instead. It first flew in September
1935, several months before the Supermarine
Spitfire that became one of its main opponents
in subsequent years. Designated in the Third
Reich's military numbering system as the Bf109,
it successfully competed against three other
designs in a competition for a new standard
Luftwaffe fighter, gaining a development contract
and going on to become widely produced.

Initial Bf109B-1 production aircraft were
delivered in February 1937. Some of these were
allocated to the Luftwaffe's premier fighter wing
JG132 'Richthofen' (named after the First World
War ace). There was an immediate opportunity
for the Bf109 to be tried out in combat. In the
Spanish Civil War air war, German-supplied and
manned Condor Legion Heinkel He51 biplanes
were hard-pressed against Spanish Republican

An immediate predecessor of the Bf109 in terms of design features and construction techniques was the Bf108 'Taifun', which was originally created as a four-seat light touring and sports aircraft. This example, Werk Nummer 2246 and civil-registered D-EBEI, is a genuine Second World War veteran that is now operated by the Deutsche Lufthansa Berlin Stiftung. *Messe-Berlin*

RIGHT: The design genius of Willy Messerschmitt and his colleagues at the Bayerische Flugzeugwerke led to the creation of the Bf109 and other notable aircraft such as the Bf108 and Bf110. Here, Messerschmitt (left) congratulates company test pilot Fritz Wendel who had just broken the world speed record for landplanes in the Me209V1, D-INJR, during April 1939. *Malcolm V. Lowe Collection*

Polikarpov I-15 biplane fighters. A small number of development Bf109s were rapidly sent to Spain, and they were followed in the spring of 1937 by a batch of operational Bf109Bs with their German pilots. There is no doubt that the subsequent success of these fighters and those that followed them were a major aid to the eventual victory of the Nationalist rebel forces in the Spanish Civil War. Thoroughly combat proven, the Bf109 in later models went on to considerable success in the Second World War.

In fact, several production models existed before the Second World War began, including the Junkers Jumo-powered Bf109B, Bf109C, and Bf109D. Towards the end of the Spanish Civil War a new and very improved Bf109 model

ABOVE: Where it all began. The very first Bf109 was the Bf109 V1, Werk Nummer 758, eventually civil-registered as D-IABI. It was powered by a 695hp Rolls-Royce Kestrel engine from Britain, and first flew in September 1935 – although it is now thought that the date might have been earlier in the year. It was flown on its first flight by Messerschmitt test pilot Hans-Dietrich Knoetzsch. *Philip Jarrett*

BELOW: A neat line-up of production Jumo-engined Bf109s greets the camera. There were very few distinguishing differences between the two types variously described as Bf109Cs and Bf109Ds, although these aircraft are actually Bf109Ds built by Focke-Wulf during 1938. *Peter Walter*

The Bf109 received its baptism of fire into aerial combat over Spain during the Spanish Civil War. Originally thought to be a Bf109B but now identified as a Bf109D of the Condor Legion's J 88 fighter unit, this Messerschmitt (coded 6-51) was usually flown by Wolfgang Schellmann. These German-flown fighters did not wear German insignia but instead bore a colour scheme adopted for Franco's so-called Spanish Nationalist rebel forces. *Philip Jarrett*

started to make its appearance in combat. This was the Bf109E, and it was this mark that was the most important fighter in service with Germany's Luftwaffe in the early Second World War period. The Bf109E introduced the Daimler-Benz DB601A inline engine of 1,100hp, and this resulted in a slightly longer fuselage and a variety of other changes compared to the Junkers

BELOW: The initial combat deployments of Bf109Bs in Spain during 1937 showed the considerable promise of the type, and the Germans were eager to combat-test new versions of the Bf109 when they became available. Here, an early Bf109E has been deployed to Spain for service with the Condor Legion and is pictured in Spanish Nationalist colours. *Philip Jarrett*

A Bf109E, coded CE+BM, on a factory test-flight prior to delivery to the Luftwaffe. Although sometimes thought of as an E-2 prototype, according to surviving company documentation this aircraft was actually a Bf109E-4. The Bf109E series introduced Daimler-Benz power to the Bf109 series in the form of the DB601 engine, in replacement of the Junkers Jumo power of the previous Bf109 production versions. *Philip Jarrett*

Jumo-engined Bf109D that went immediately before it. The Bf109E started to reach Luftwaffe units in 1939, the so-called Munich Agreement between Britain, France and Germany of 1938 having given the Germans a good breathing space to continue their rearmament.

By the start of the Second World War the Bf109E had almost completely replaced the Bf109D in front-line Luftwaffe units (although some Bf109Ds were still involved in combat over Poland in September 1939 alongside the Bf109E). The Bf109E was produced by a variety of manufacturers at various locations in Germany, to the tune of several distinct fighter

RIGHT: The Bf109E was the mainstay of the Luftwaffe's early Second World War campaigns and was highly successful against all fighter opposition that it met – except when faced by the Supermarine Spitfire and Hawker Hurricane. *Peter Walter*

and fighter-bomber models. It was involved in all the Luftwaffe's early Second World War campaigns, including service in North Africa where specially-configured 'tropicalised' models were in combat. They were far superior to much of the fighter opposition they faced in the early war years, with the notable and very important exceptions of the British Hawker Hurricane and especially the Supermarine Spitfire.

The Bf109E was the main German fighter type during the Battle of Britain, but an Achilles heel of the Bf109 in all its various marks was a lack of range, and this was an important factor in the Luftwaffe's eventual defeat in the Battle of Britain. Nevertheless, the Bf109E was well-liked by its pilots (despite it being small and cramped, and often ground-looping due to its narrow-track main undercarriage), and many fighter pilots achieved fame and (for some) a considerable string of victories while at its controls. They included such legendary flyers as Adolf Galland, Johannes Steinhoff and Josef Priller, and some of these pilots were among the top-scoring fighter aces of all time.

A considerable advantage for the Bf109 over the Spitfire was the inclusion of fuel-injection for its Daimler-Benz engine, allowing it the luxury of inverted flight for longer than the Spitfire with its carburettor-fed Rolls-Royce Merlin engine – although this problem was addressed in later versions of the Spitfire. Export customers for the Bf109E included such countries as Switzerland and Yugoslavia, and the type started to equip fighter units in several countries of Eastern Europe that were sympathetic to the German cause.

Partly in an effort to keep the Bf109 competitive with developments introduced on the Supermarine Spitfire, a major improvement of the Bf109 was attempted with the Bf109F model. This refined version included a redesigned wing of different span and configuration, in addition to various other changes. Deliveries to the Luftwaffe started in 1941, and among the various production models there was a dedicated reconnaissance version with cameras installed.

June 1941 saw the commencement of the German invasion of the Soviet Union. From the start, the Bf109 was a central part of the Luftwaffe's aerial strategy in the operations against the Soviet Union. Some of

ABOVE: An RAF pilot examines the tailplane of a shot down Bf109E-4, Werk Nummer 5587. The Messerschmitt, Yellow 10, belonged to 6./JG 51, and was brought down in August 1940 during the Battle of Britain at East Langdon, Kent. It was subsequently stripped by souvenir hunters. *Malcolm V. Lowe Collection*

BELOW: A neat line-up of wrecked and captured Bf109s in North Africa, believed to have been photographed near to Gambut. Large numbers of Bf109s were abandoned by the retreating German forces in North Africa and it was here that Black 6, the focus of this book, fell into Allied hands. *Philip Jarrett*

the greatest air battles ever seen took place in the subsequent struggle, and the Luftwaffe amassed the largest number of aerial victories ever recorded over what became known as the Eastern Front. Operations in Russia were on an enormous scale, and the Bf109 was at the centre of events on the Eastern Front to the very end of the war.

Continuing development led to the later Bf109G and Bf109K models, and these two persisted in Luftwaffe service through to the finale of the Second World War, with production and recycling of earlier airframes continuing at the end. This was achieved despite the widespread utilisation of Germany's other main Second World War, single-engine fighter, the Focke-Wulf Fw190, which entered service in the late summer of 1941. The Bf109G was a developed version of the Bf109F, powered by the Daimler-Benz DB605 inline engine with some versions featuring a crude form of 'pressurisation'. The Bf109G also included considerable weight escalation due to the need to equip these aircraft with an increasing array of weapons to counter Allied fighters and heavy bombers. The first production sub-types, the Bf109G-1 and G-2, entered service during 1942. More Bf109G were built than any other mark of Bf109, and there was a wealth of different versions and sub-types, including some

ABOVE: An early Bf109G, probably a Bf109G-0 pre-production aircraft, has its DB605 engine test-run. Access to the engine on all Bf109s was very good, with cowling panels easily removed and most of the important equipment comparatively easy to hand. *Philip Jarrett*

BELOW: Operating conditions in the Soviet Union were often poor, and sometimes terrible. This Bf109G-2 of 5./JG 54 is seen wading through mud at an airfield during the ultimately disastrous Russian campaign. The Bf109 was a difficult aircraft to take-off and land at the best of times, but in conditions like these the Luftwaffe pilots needed to be particularly careful. Nevertheless, the Bf109 was very successful in the skies over Russia, particularly in the early stages of the German invasion. *Philip Jarrett*

fitted with wooden tails to ease manufacturing considerations. The Bf109G served on all the war fronts where the Luftwaffe was active, and was involved in trying (increasingly unsuccessfully) to counter the daylight bombing raids on Germany and Occupied Europe by American heavy bombers with their deadly escort fighters. A two-seat trainer version of the G-series, the Bf109G-12, was also built. Continued development led to the Bf109K, the final major production version which was starting to serve in numbers at the end of the war.

Among the many famous German pilots who flew the Bf109 in combat was Erich Hartmann, who is the highest-scoring fighter ace of all time with 352 victories – although it must be stressed that not all claims necessarily represented actual losses on the opposing side. Many of Germany's allies also flew the Bf109, including notably Hungary (together with licence-production), Romania, Croatia, Slovakia, Italy and Finland.

The type's combat career did not end with the Second World War. Originally combat-tested in the Spanish Civil War, the Bf109 was much-liked by the Spanish who built it as the Hispano Buchón powered by the Rolls-Royce Merlin engine (which normally powered the Bf109's great rival, the Supermarine Spitfire). Spanish Buchóns served into the mid-1960s. In post-war Czechoslovakia, the type was built as the Avia S-199 (and CS-199 two-seater) with locally-configured Junkers Jumo 211

power, some of these flying for Israel in that country's fight against its Arab neighbours in the later 1940s. In total some 35,000 examples of Bf109s of all types were built (exact figures are impossible to verify), including production by several other companies in addition to Messerschmitt. This impressive number was second only to the Soviet Union's Ilyushin Il-2 'Shturmovik' attack aircraft.

Nevertheless, despite the undoubted prowess of the Bf109, particularly in the early stages of the Second World War, it still ended

Classic aircraft preservation

There is a great fascination for all things aviation, especially historic aviation, and both modern and historic aircraft draw their own supporters at the many air shows and museums across the country.

From the beginning of aviation history there has been little thought given to the preservation of the aircraft that have preceded the newer, more effective models. Each generation has looked to the future, rather than preserving the past for future generations to learn from and enjoy.

Now people are more interested in history; in tracing their forebears and in understanding the history that goes hand in hand with them. The importance of classic aircraft has grown and with it the responsibility to preserve the few examples that we still have of our aviation history.

The aircraft, whether it's a biplane or a large four-engined bomber, reflect the development, the engineering of the day and, if they're flying, ensure that the grace of the aerial performance is kept alive for future generations.

ABOVE: What it's really all about: the sight and sound of a historic aircraft in the air is priceless. Bf109G-10/Buchón composite, D-FDME, Black 2, operated by the Messerschmitt Stiftung (Foundation) and EADS at Manching, Germany, displays the genuine grace of the Bf109. *Messe-Berlin*

up on the losing side. No Bf109s remained operational after the end of the Second World War in any numbers except in Spain and Finland (although moves were made to continue to employ the type in Italy). On the contrary, many thousands of ex-Luftwaffe Bf109s were scrapped by the victorious Allies in the months after the end of the war, and the type slowly disappeared into history, largely but not totally forgotten. This shaped the Bf109's post-war life and the public's perception of the type, particularly in Western Europe and the US. Although construction took place of Bf109 derivatives after the end of the war, this was in Czechoslovakia and Spain – both closed societies under dictatorships about which very little was known in the West. A comparatively small number of Bf109s went on display in museums around the world in the post-war period, but the type was perceived as having been on the losing side. In comparison, the successful aircraft of the Second World War period that were employed by the Allies, such as the Supermarine Spitfire, tended to stay in the public's mind, and remained much better known to those on the 'winning side'. Airworthy examples of the Spitfire continued to persist, while the Bf109 was effectively grounded, with no flyable examples extant in the West and certainly none appearing in the air at air shows, or special events like those to commemorate the Battle of Britain.

This perception changed from the later 1960s. Probably the one single event that raised the status of the Bf109 in the minds of the public was the making of a film. The *Battle of Britain* brought together a most unusual collection of what were coming to be called 'warbirds' – airworthy Second World War aircraft, owned and operated by private individuals or companies outside any sort of official or military ownership. Under the energetic direction of retired RAF Group Captain Hamish Mahaddie, a strange mix of RAF and 'Luftwaffe' aircraft was brought together in 1967 and 1968 for the making of the movie, which loosely told the story of the Battle of Britain in 1940. The film included spectacular aerial sequences – mainly shot from a specially converted North American B-25 Mitchell – that really caught the public's imagination. The RAF

LEFT: Four Hispano Buchóns masquerade as Bf109Es during the making of the film 'Battle of Britain' during 1968. This film was a landmark for the awakening 'warbird' movement and encouraged the growing interest in keeping historic aircraft alive and airworthy. Of the aircraft illustrated in this formation, 'Red 7' is still airworthy and flies as G-BWUE. It is owned by Spitfire Ltd and is based at Duxford in Cambridgeshire.
Malcolm V. Lowe Collection

aircraft were quite genuine, comprising a mix of Spitfires and less numerous Hawker Hurricanes – although many of the Spitfires were actually of later marks than those that fought in the real Battle of Britain. The 'Luftwaffe' aircraft, however, were a real surprise. At that time there were no airworthy Bf109s anywhere in the world, nor any flyable German-built bombers from the 1940s. However, during that period the Spanish air force was retiring its Hispano HA-1112-M1L Buchón fighters (derivatives of the Bf109G) and CASA-built Heinkel He111 bomber lookalikes. Although the bulky Merlin installation in the Buchóns looked distinctly un-Messerschmitt like, they proved to be admirable stand-ins for early war Bf109Es that would have fought in the Battle of Britain.

In total, over 20 Buchóns were purchased at auction from the Spanish by Spitfire Productions Ltd for the making of the film. They needed some cosmetic surgery to make them look like Bf109Es and so their wing-tips were squared-off, the distinctive Bf109E tail struts were added and dummy machine guns were installed in the wings in Bf109E-style. The filming began in Spain, but later 17 of the Buchóns were flown via France to Duxford in Cambridgeshire. During the summer of 1968, the Buchóns, 2 CASA-built Heinkel He111 lookalikes and several Spitfires and Hurricanes were flown by specially-commissioned pilots in mock dogfights over the countryside of East Anglia and southern England.

When released in 1969 the movie was an instant success, and its real stars were the aircraft. There can be no doubt that historic aircraft preservation, and particularly the desire to retain in flyable condition examples such as the Spitfire, received a real shot in the arm as a result of this one single event. Although the Hispano Buchóns in the film did an admirable job in making the Bf109 a more high-profile type to a new generation of enthusiasts, there remained no airworthy examples of genuine Bf109s – although some of the Hispano Buchóns that starred in the film were sold on and continue to be flyable.

The possibility of a genuine Bf109 being made airworthy eventually became a reality by the almost single-handed actions and single-mindedness of one man – Russ Snadden. As explained later in this book, he was responsible, together with a similarly dedicated team of helpers, of returning to airworthy condition the former Luftwaffe Bf109G-2 Black 6. This restoration took the best part of two decades, and was done on a personal initiative basis, with no specific or long-term official assistance, even though the aircraft was and remains

ABOVE: Much work is needed to make a Hispano Buchón into a Bf109G-look-alike, particular on the nose area. This Buchón masquerading as a Bf109G-2 in the Luftwaffenmuseum, at the former RAF Gatow airfield on the outskirts of Berlin, is a very convincing reconstruction, with realistic-looking nose contours and engine cowlings for the DB605A engine.
Malcolm V. Lowe

government-owned property – having been captured in North Africa in 1942, and never sold on to private owners. Getting this aircraft back into the air was a fantastic achievement, even though it was always officially intended that it would be allowed to fly for just a few years. Sadly it was badly damaged on its last flight in 1997, and needed a considerable amount of work to be made fit for static display.

Despite the success of Russ Snadden and his colleagues in returning Black 6 to airworthy condition in the early 1990s, there was no sudden upsurge in the numbers of flyable Bf109s. All museum examples remained in place, the expense and difficulty in obtaining suitable spares and expertise for making these aircraft airworthy rendering the prospect unlikely in every case. Nevertheless, the opening up of the former Soviet Union at the end of the Cold War resulted in a number of interesting Second World War airframes being rescued from their crash sites. This has included several Messerschmitts, and a small trickle of Bf109s has started to reach airworthy condition, albeit

thanks to private initiative and the expenditure of large sums of money. Just how genuine some of these aircraft really are, bearing in mind that virtually everything has to be replaced and new components made to make them airworthy, is open to debate. Indeed, there are some who would prefer ground-up restorations of that type to be called replicas containing some original parts, rather than their being considered to be genuine restored historic aircraft.

However, a level of interest has continued to exist in the Hispano Buchón, three decades after the making of the *Battle of Britain*. At the time of writing a handful of these Spanish-built Bf109 lookalikes remain airworthy or potentially airworthy. They include the closely-guarded trio operated in some secrecy by the Willy Messerschmitt Stiftung in Germany in conjunction with the European multi-national aviation-manufacturing and space group EADS. These aircraft have been re-engined with Daimler-Benz DB605 engines and therefore look like genuine Bf109Gs, one of them including some genuine Bf109G parts in its airframe.

What's in a name?

There exists to this day some confusion as to the correct nomenclature to use with regard to the 109. During the Second World War this aircraft type was known to the Allies almost universally as the Messerschmitt Me109. This was not the correct terminology and it was always intended to be designated correctly by the Germans as the Bf109. This stemmed from the fact that its design originated in the days of Bayerische Flugzeugwerke AG, and hence the 'Bf' abbreviation was correct for the '109, just as it was for other contemporary types from that company such as the Bf108 single-engine light transport and touring monoplane and Bf110 twin-engined destroyer/heavy fighter. After the passing of Bayerische Flugzeugwerke in July 1938 and its replacement by Messerschmitt AG, all subsequent types that originated with the new concern were designated 'Me' – such as the Me262 late-war twin-engined jet fighter. Data plates on Bf109s almost always refer to the aircraft as a Bf109, although it is interesting to note that on some original German documents of the Second World War period the term 'Me109' was occasionally used.

During the spring of 1937 the first Bf109B-1s were delivered to the Luftwaffe fighter wing Jagdgeschwader 132 'Richthofen' under the command of Oberst Gerd von Massow. It was the start of a long and very hard-fought career. This was the first production model of a fighter which, more than any other aircraft, the name of Messerschmitt is associated.

BELOW: The aircraft is a Bf109G-6/R6 (sometimes claimed to be a G-5) from the 7th Staffel of fighter wing JG27. The Bf109G-5 and G-6 were significant production models of the Bf109 line in the 1943 period onwards, although many pilots felt that the Bf109 was past its best by that point. Nevertheless, the type persisted in production and service and continued to be a central part of the Luftwaffe's war effort. *Malcolm V. Lowe Collection*

Chapter One

The Bf109 story

Dating back to the earliest days of the Nazi regime in Germany, the far-reaching specifications that led to the creation of the Bf109 showed the German aircraft industry's willingness to embrace advanced thinking in aircraft design and construction. It resulted in the Bf109 being well ahead of most of its potential opponents when it entered front-line service in 1937.

LEFT: Production of the Bf109 reached the staggering figure of well over 30,000 examples. This was achieved by the parent company in conjunction with a series of other aircraft manufacturers and associated sub-contractors. Here Bf109G manufacture is under way. As the war progressed, manufacturing became increasingly disrupted and dispersed due to Allied bombing. This view of a crowded production room contrasts with the vast uninterrupted assembly halls and moving production lines of gleaming fighters and bombers under construction, characteristic of aircraft production in the United States. *Messerschmitt AG*

When it was designed in the mid-1930s, the Bf109 was one of the most advanced warplanes of its day. Willy Messerschmitt and his fellow designers embraced many of the new concepts that were coming to the fore in fighter aircraft design for their new fighter project. These included the low-wing cantilever monoplane layout, all-metal stressed skin construction, and the use of a modern, high-performance (for its day) inline piston engine. The whole design of the Bf109 was clean and well thought out. It was a world away from the heavily-rigged, canvas-covered biplane fighters that many nations were at that time still using as front-line equipment.

The Bf109 dated from a specification released as far back as 1933. In that year the Nazis successfully gained power in Germany, what they then called the Third Reich, and at once set about modernising and massively expanding the German armed forces. The new RLM (Reichsluftfahrtministerium, the Third Reich's aviation ministry) issued a demanding requirement in July 1933 calling for a new and advanced single-seat fighter, with a number of specific qualities. In addition to the normal requirements for a fighter of its day, one quirk was the need for the planned aircraft to be transportable by rail. No mention was made of wing armament or of long range/endurance. These realities were of great importance in determining the size, design and armament layout of the new fighter. The Bf109's

BELOW: A number of prototype/test aircraft were built to develop the Bf109 line, including the third aircraft known as the V3 and civil-registered as D-IOQY. Powered by a Junkers Jumo 210 engine, this and several other early trials Bf109s were used for development of the Jumo-engined layout, which was initially series-produced as the Bf109B, C and D versions. This aircraft also trialled the armament layout of two MG17 machine guns in the upper forward fuselage, with a centrally-mounted weapon in the so-called 'motor cannon' or 'engine-mounted' installation. *Philip Jarrett*

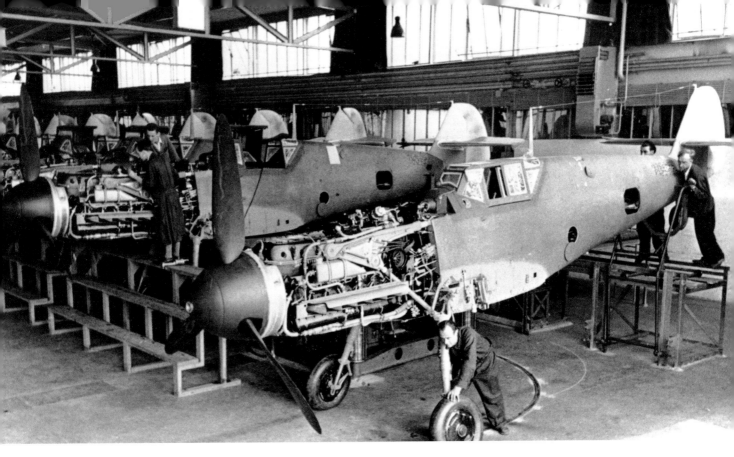

narrow-track main undercarriage, which from the beginning caused so many problems to its pilots on take-off and landing, was a result of the requirement for the aircraft to be rail transportable – as designed and manufactured, the undercarriage of all Bf109s was attached to the fuselage, allowing the wings to be easily removed while the fuselage stood on its undercarriage, causing its track to be extremely narrow.

Four manufacturers responded with prototypes to the July 1933 requirement. The design from Willy Messerschmitt and his colleagues at the Bayerische Flugzeugwerke AG was victorious, although one of the rivals, the Heinkel He112, was a good contender that was also eventually series produced, mainly for export. That Messerschmitt succeeded at all was a breakthrough, because some in the Third Reich's hierarchy had a profound dislike for him and his designs.

Following the successful first flight in September 1935 the Bf109 showed great promise, and series production was initiated with the first production aircraft entering service in early 1937. It went from strength to strength, and proved at once to be a war-winner – the contribution of the early Bf109s that were sent to Spain and flown by German 'volunteer' pilots in support of General Franco's rebel forces resulted during 1939 in the first major

ABOVE: A production line view of Bf109Gs showing the main undercarriage attachment to the fuselage. This was a most unusual arrangement for a contemporary fighter and resulted in the Bf109's main undercarriage having a very narrow track, which in turn led to problems when landing or taking off under less than ideal conditions. *Messerschmitt AG*

BELOW: The Bf109B commenced combat operations in Spain during the first half of 1937 wearing Spanish Nationalist colours, but flown by German pilots. This particular Bf109B landed at a Spanish government-held airfield and aroused great interest not just for the Spanish Republicans but for many other countries as well. *Philip Jarrett*

Fascist victory in warfare. The initial austere, but nonetheless capable, Junkers Jumo-powered Bf109 versions, give way on the production lines during 1938 to the Daimler-Benz powered Bf109E, which was the major fighter type with which the Luftwaffe went to war in September 1939 against Poland in the opening days of the Second World War. The contribution of the Bf109 during that conflict cannot be overestimated. It fought on all fronts for the Luftwaffe, and in the early days was tremendously successful, being a quantum leap ahead of any opponents that it faced. It subsequently played a key role in the Battle of Britain, but in that arena it was faced by modern fighters for the first time in any numbers, and could not defeat the RAF's Spitfires and Hurricanes. During the German invasion of the Soviet Union in June 1941 it reigned supreme for several months, although from the late summer it was increasingly partnered by the excellent radial-engine Focke-Wulf Fw190. The Bf109 was essentially the backbone of the Luftwaffe's fighter arm in the Second World War and it is the one aircraft type with which the name of Messerschmitt will always be associated.

The Germans specialised in the provision of 'add-on' equipment sets, which were made available for attachment to several different

Luftwaffe warplanes, including the Bf109 (particularly from the Bf109F series onwards), to improve performance or firepower for specific missions. There were Rüstsatz (R) conversion kits for installation in the field, such as add-on armament options, and Umrüst-Bausatz (U) sets that were installed at the factory to allow a specific capability or armament option that could not be easily added in the field. As the war started to turn against the Germans, so the Bf109 became more important, even though it was slowly losing its pre-eminence as better Allied fighters started making their appearance.

The number of roles that the Bf109 fulfilled grew longer as the war continued, with fighter, fighter-bomber, and fighter-reconnaissance being among the most important. Some were even tried out as night-fighters under the 'Wilde Sau' (Wild Boar) project to counter RAF night bombers in 1943. Bf109s on home defence duties fought a long duel with high-flying US heavy bombers and their increasingly deadly escort fighters, with the Bf109s sometimes flying cover for heavily-armed Fw190s – the Messerschmitts taking on the US fighters while the Fw190s went after the bombers. In the final days of the war Bf109s were pressed into last-ditch ground-attack missions against Soviet ground targets, but the end of the war saw

ABOVE: The Bf109 was operated to great effect in North Africa, where Germany came to the aid of its Fascist partner Italy. Here a late mark Bf109E, possibly an E-7, is serviced by the tireless and hard-working ground personnel. 'Tropicalised' versions of the Bf109, with sand filters for key air intakes, were developed for this type of environment, which was harsh on man and machine. *Philip Jarrett*

BELOW: A Bf109F of JG54 is man-handled into cover by several ground personnel on the Eastern Front. Luftwaffe Bf109 pilots achieved an enormous number of aerial victories over Soviet aircraft during the war in the east, although an examination of Soviet records made available following the end of the Cold War suggests that many claims were exaggerated. *Philip Jarrett*

ABOVE: **A posed propaganda photograph that nevertheless yields some useful details of the Bf109G series. The aircraft is a Bf109G-5 and has the characteristic 'square' heavily-framed cockpit canopy of the early to mid-production Bf109Gs, before that heavy and cumbersome fitting was replaced by the 'Erla Haube' of later marks. The supercharger air intake on the port cowling is also prominent, and the split inner flap arrangement is also visible.** *Philip Jarrett*

large numbers of Bf109s all over the defeated Third Reich, the vast majority of which were soon scrapped.

Manufacture of the Bf109 was undertaken by the parent company, and a considerable number of sub-contractors. As one of the giants of the German aviation industry, Messerschmitt was at the head of a large organisation that oversaw Bf109 sub-contracting and final assembly throughout the Third Reich and its occupied territories. Messerschmitt's own facilities at Regensburg were a prime contractor, but various other locations included Wiener-Neustadt in Austria. Companies such as Arado and Erla assembled Messerschmitts – Black 6, the main focus of this book, was a Bf109G-2 built by Erla Maschinenwerk GmbH of Leipzig, actually at Leipzig-Mockau. A sometimes quoted figure for wartime production (September 1939–May 1945) of the Bf109 is 30,573 examples, although record-keeping was non-existent by May 1945 and so this total should be viewed with some scepticism.

Variations on a theme

Bf109 versions

The Third Reich was well-known for its meticulous record keeping. This gives us a very precise view of Bf109 production in the

early days, from the Bf109B right up to the early versions of the Bf109G. Later in the war Allied bombing increasingly disrupted production, necessitating dispersal of production and sub-contracting. This precipitated the process of poor record keeping that has considerably clouded the picture of later Bf109 production. The Allied bombing also disrupted the work of bureaucrats in a more general sense, allowing for this increasingly poor record keeping to become an even greater problem. The exact number of Bf109s built is impossible to determine due to the loss of key documents at the war's end, and the fragmentary nature of production in the final months. Additionally, it must be remembered that towards the end of the war many 'completed' airframes were not combat ready or even airworthy. The almost complete disruption of the shrinking Third Reich's transportation network in the concluding stages of the war, which caused supplies of parts and sub-contracted components to be disrupted and often not delivered, combined with petrol shortages and other difficulties, meant that many Bf109s were not able to join combat, even though official RLM documents might have suggested otherwise. Even aircraft that were delivered to front-line units were often found to be missing key equipment, necessitating unit-level modification work before they could be considered ready for action. Added to this deteriorating situation was the sabotage of some airframes particularly in dispersed production sites, where foreign labourers were pressed into working for the Third Reich and were often more likely to sabotage components rather than finish them to a high standard.

The following is a brief listing of the principal German-built production versions of the Bf109. More thorough details of the weapons and power plants fitted in these different models are given elsewhere in the book.

Bf109A

A short series of seven pre-production Bf109s was built, tentatively designated Bf109A, with Jumo 210 power. Two early prototype/development aircraft, which were evaluated in Spain from November 1936 are also sometimes referred to as 'Bf109A' airframes.

Showing off its purposeful lines, an early production Bf109B is seen at Messerschmitt's Augsburg factory airfield. Initial Bf109Bs could be identified by the addition of an aerial wire extending from the radio mast to each horizontal tail surface as seen here.
Philip Jarrett

Bf109B

The Bf109B was the first major Bf109 production series, with carburettor-equipped Jumo 210D power and simple two-machine gun armament. Early Bf109Bs were fitted with a wooden Schwarz two-bladed fixed-pitch propeller, later production examples had VDM two-bladed variable-pitch propeller units (there was no differentiation by sub-type in Messerschmitt documents to tell between

them). This version saw action early in its operational life in Spain during the first half of 1937. It is confirmed that 344 were built, the Third Reich's record-keeping at that time being untroubled by wartime conditions.

Bf109C

Similar to the basic Bf109B series, but with various detail improvements and an increase in internal fuel, as well as the addition of

LEFT: The Bf109B was the first major production version of the Bf109 series, and was combat evaluated in the Spanish Civil War. This view of a Condor Legion Bf109B gives a good impression of the general layout of the early Bf109s. Particularly notable is the generous wing flap area, which was retained for subsequent production versions of the Bf109 until the Bf109F and later production models, when split wing flaps of different proportions were introduced.
Philip Jarrett

BELOW: A Bf109C or D in Condor Legion service in Spain. The Bf109C introduced wing gun armament into the Bf109 series, even though the wing of the Bf109 had not been designed for internal armament. Early experience in combat over Spain with the lightly-armed Bf109B, which did not carry wing guns, showed that the Bf109 needed to be up-gunned with wing gun armament. *Philip Jarrett*

wing-mounted machine guns (one in each wing in the C-1 version) which the Bf109 had not been designed to carry. The Jumo 210G fuel-injection engine was fitted. Only 58 Bf109Cs were built.

Bf109D

The final Jumo-powered Bf109 version was the Bf109D, fitted with the carburettor-equipped Jumo 210D engine. This model included the detail improvements of the Bf109C and included the four machine gun armament of the Bf109C-1. A total of 657 of these still somewhat austere but nevertheless capable fighters were built.

Bf109E

The first major version of the Bf109 to be really combat-ready to take on high-performance

fighters such as the Spitfire, the Bf109E or 'Emil' represented a major step forward in Bf109 design. It was the first Bf109 version to be Daimler-Benz powered, using the supercharged DB 601 series. The entire forward fuselage was redesigned, the supercharger air intake relocated from the upper right-hand cowling of the Jumo-powered Messerschmitts to a new mid-position on the left-hand side of the engine cowling, and

many detail changes were made to equipment. The large lower nose radiator for engine coolant of the Jumo-engine versions was moved to a new underwing position, and was replaced by a shallower lower-nose oil radiator. A three-bladed, VDM variable-pitch metal propeller unit was now standard.

There was a large variety of sub-variants within the Bf109E manufacture, starting with

ABOVE: The early Jumo-engined Bf109 series were the first major monoplane fighters to reach the Luftwaffe in numbers. They continued to be important even after the service debut of the DB601-engined Bf109E series, with some serving briefly as night-fighters in 1940. This is a Jumo-powered Bf109C or D. *Philip Jarrett*

LEFT: A rather untidily upended Bf109E, in a pose all too characteristic for the type. *Malcolm V. Lowe Collection*

ABOVE: Detail of the braced horizontal tailplane of the Bf109E series, a feature discontinued from the Bf109F onwards. The aircraft pictured is Bf109E-4, Werk Nummer 1480, of the headquarters (Stab.) of II./JG 3, and was being flown by Oberleutnant Franz von Werra when it was brought down in Kent on 5 September 1940. Von Werra is generally regarded to have been the only Axis prisoner of war to escape from a Canadian prison camp and return to Germany. *Malcolm V. Lowe Collection*

BELOW: A considerable amount of redesign work went into the Bf109 series to create the Bf109F production model. The layout was pioneered on several Versuchs machines, including this aircraft, VK+AB, sometimes referred to as a Bf109F-0 or the Bf109V24. The Bf109F series eventually emerged as a radical makeover of the Bf109 line, with the DB601 engine layout successfully able to carry a centrally-located weapon, and many detail changes including the deletion of the horizontal tail struts and the alteration of the wings with the introduction of rounded wing tips, although these were not trialled on the aircraft illustrated here. *Philip Jarrett*

the Bf109E-1 and continuing to the E-8. This showed the growing versatility of the Bf109 series, as fighter-bomber variations were introduced with the provision of under-fuselage weapons carriage, and camera-equipped reconnaissance models also made their appearance. Range and endurance were additionally improved with the provision for a 300-litre jettisonable fuel tank beneath the fuselage.

During the Bf109E series a new, square framed cockpit canopy was introduced that replaced the more rounded shape of previous versions. Factory-installed armour plate within the canopy for the pilot's head was included from the Bf109E-4 onwards. A 'tropical' version for use in hot sandy or dust-laden environments was also introduced, with the installation of a dust or sand filter to fit on to the supercharger air intake. The Bf109E was very widely manufactured, and was produced from late 1938 onwards, entering widespread Luftwaffe service during the first half of 1939.

Bf109F

Although the Bf109E represented a major upgrading of the capability and performance of the Bf109 series, the Bf109F, or Friedrich, was an even more radical alteration to the basic Bf109 layout. Many changes were made to systems and equipment, some equipment and filler points were relocated, and the basic shape of the aircraft was altered. The cooling and hydraulic systems were redesigned, the nose was somewhat more streamlined even though the DB 601-series engine type was retained for the Bf109F line, and armament within the wings was deleted for good. A successful engine-mounted centrally-located weapon installation was also introduced for the Friedrich series. The wing was redesigned, and the distinctive rounded wing-tips of the later production Bf109s were introduced. The equally distinctive horizontal tail bracing struts of the Bf109E and earlier series were done away with, but initially this appeared to have caused some accidents with tail assemblies breaking away in flight, leading to a temporary stiffening of the tail-to-fuselage join with external strengthening strips until a factory internal strengthening layout could be devised.

There were also many smaller changes – the pilot's seat, for example, was altered in design but from then onwards needed to be adjusted on the ground if necessary before the pilot was on board. Other alterations, such as wider propeller blades and a changed supercharger air intake profile, plus a deepened intake under the nose for the oil cooler, set apart the final Bf109F-4 version from earlier Bf109Fs, some of which were upgraded. As with the Bf109E series, there were a number of fighter-bomber sub-types.

Approximately 3,428 Bf109Fs were built, including pre-production development examples, and the Friedrich was initially introduced into Luftwaffe service in September/October 1940, with production continuing into May 1942.

Bf109G

Many German pilots considered the Bf109F series to be the zenith of Bf109 development, before weight increases and add-ons with the Bf109G versions degraded performance. The Bf109G, or Gustav series, included the addition of the DB 605-series engine, the widespread use of power boost systems (GM 1 and MW 50), and the introduction of pressurised versions (the G-1, G-3 and G-5), which included a somewhat crude early form of sealed pressurised cockpit for high-altitude combat against US bombers. But only some 700 of those were built. The Bf109G included the improvements of the Bf109F series, but there were many detail changes with the Gustav, among the more obvious being a heavier cockpit canopy and windscreen with increased armour, and the widespread but not universal use of under-wing armament in add-on sets. A very noticeable addition to the engine cowling was a pronounced new bulge on each side from the Bf109G-6 and G-6 onwards, due to the up-gunning of this version with heavier machine guns in the upper forward fuselage. Later sub-types were fitted with more powerful DB 605/AS engines with a different supercharger, which necessitated a further major modification to the cowling shape, which was wider and more streamlined. As with the Bf109E series, there were a number of fighter-bomber and reconnaissance sub-types.

Manufacture of the Gustav series took pace from 1942 onwards, with the initial Bf109G-1

ABOVE: A line-up of newly-completed Bf109G-1 production aircraft in 1942 prior to delivery. Each aircraft bears the four-digit factory code letters or radio call sign (Stammkennzeichen) on the fuselage – these were usually painted out on receipt by an operational unit and appropriate unit-level markings applied instead. Each aircraft wears the camouflage scheme of mid-war greys typical of Bf109s destined for combat units in North-West Europe or on the Russian Front. *Philip Jarrett*

BELOW: A number of Bf109s fell into Allied hands as the Second World War progressed, some of which were still flyable and in a condition suitable for evaluation. One of these was the Bf109G-1, Werk Nummer 413598, shown here. It was captured at the Dutch airfield of Gilze-Rijen and flown to England in February 1945, having been painted in British camouflage colours with 'invasion stripes' beneath the wings. Allocated the British military serial number VD358 in April 1945, it was flown by the Enemy Aircraft Flight of the Central Fighter Establishment at RAF Tangmere and coded 'EA-2', but its eventual fate is not clear. It was fitted with the 'clear vision' Erla Haube cockpit cover as used by many late-war Bf109s. *Philip Jarrett*

and G-2 entering service in June 1942. Black 6 was of the G-2 sub-type. Later production of the Bf109G took place against the backdrop of the deteriorating war situation in Germany, and manufacturing standards accordingly suffered. Some later Gustavs were fitted with tall wooden tails, partly to relieve demand for metal products, there eventually being several slightly different types of vertical tail due to the fragmented nature of late-war manufacture. The last version of the Bf109 that was produced in the Second World War was the G-10.

The exact number of Bf109Gs that were built is impossible to determine, but it was certainly many thousands, the Gustav being the most numerous of the whole Bf109 line.

Bf109K

Delays with advanced fighter projects such as the Me262 jet fighter resulted in Bf109 manufacture continuing longer than had been anticipated by the Luftwaffe, and the Bf109K arose partly from the need to continue with Bf109 production but also to improve the breed. The resulting Bf109K series was similar to the late-war Bf109G production sub-types, and included the use of wood for its

tail surfaces similar to the pattern established in late Bf109G production – which continued concurrent with Bf109K manufacture. Although several production versions of the Bf109K were planned, only the Bf109K-4 is known to have entered service from late 1944 (probably October or November). This sub-type was armed from the start with the heaviest weapon to be fitted within the Bf109 airframe, the MK108 30mm cannon (although some Gustavs also had this weapon installed) in the centrally-located engine-mounted position. Production totals for the Bf109K are impossible to determine.

Two-seater Bf109s

The difficulties of flying the Bf109 due to its cramped cockpit, poor outside vision behind and down, and particularly its less than forgiving antics while taking-off and landing, have already been touched on elsewhere in this book. The situation was recognised by Messerschmitt and the Luftwaffe as being sufficiently serious to result in the development of a dedicated two-seater trainer version of the Bf109 series, the Bf109G-12. The version was created from conversions of existing Bf109G-2, G-4 and G-6

BELOW: Production of the Bf109 during the latter stages of the Second World War included the later marks of the Bf109G series, and the Bf109K. Displaying many of the attributes of the late production Bf109, this aircraft has been variously described as a Bf109K-4 or Bf109G-10 (it is almost certainly the former), and wore the foreign evaluation number T2-123. It was photographed in the US after the end of the Second World War.
Philip Jarrett

airframes and was not a new-build mark – the aircraft so converted retained their original Werk Nummern. The work was carried out by Blohm & Voss at Hamburg and resulted in 494 known conversions being made up to December 1944 when record-keeping and the war situation slowed or stopped the programme.

The new rear cockpit was fitted with dual controls and was for the instructor, with the pupil pilot seated in the normal front seat. Each cockpit was fitted with its own sideways-hinged cockpit canopy. The forward view of the instructor in the rear seat was severely limited, resulting in the side windows of his opening canopy being set outwards in a multi-panel arrangement for slightly improved vision. A periscope was provided for the instructor in the rear seat but was in practice just about useless. He spoke with the pupil pilot by means of an internal intercom system. The Bf109's already limited fuel capacity was further reduced due to the addition of the rear cockpit, with only 235 litres being carried (compared to the nominal 400 litres available to the normal single-seat fighter versions), although a 300-litre under-fuselage drop tank could be carried as the Bf109G-12/R3. It is not clear how

effective these trainers were, but in post-war Czechoslovakia a two-seat conversion was also carried out by Avia as the CS-199 to go alongside the single-seat re-engined CS-99 fighters that were made there.

The well-known British test pilot Lieutenant (later Captain) Eric 'Winkle' Brown flew a captured Bf109G-12 on one occasion. Somewhat dangerously, he flew it alone, sitting in the rear cockpit, in order to ascertain what kind of visibility and control the rear-seat occupant (the instructor) normally had. He soon discovered that this plan was not a good idea, and found it almost impossible to fly the aircraft safely, let alone land it. Visibility over the Bf109's nose was never good for landing or ground taxiing, but from the back seat of the G-12's rearward-extended cockpit it was just about zero. He was able to execute a difficult and nerve-racking landing on the third attempt, and did not try the manoeuvre again.

Other versions

A number of other Bf109 versions were planned, envisaged or built in small numbers. These included the Bf109T based on the Bf109E-7/N but with extended wing span, a

BELOW: A two-seat operational conversion trainer version of the Bf109, the G-12, was developed by Messerschmitt later in the war to help the transition of novice pilots onto the type, and to allow familiarisation with the Bf109's difficult take-off and landing characteristics. Bf109V52, CJ+MG, pioneered the conversion. The new two-seat layout placed the instructor in the rear seat with virtually no forward vision, hence the outward-extended glazing of this new crew position. *Philip Jarrett*

tail-hook mounted beneath the rear fuselage, and catapult fittings, which was intended to operate from the German aircraft carrier *Graf Zeppelin*. This ship was never completed and the 79 Bf109T built were subsequently used as land-based fighters. The Bf109Z was a bizarre concept that would have mated two Bf109 fuselages with a common central wing section to create a twin fuselage contraption – it was never flown. The Bf109X designation has sometimes been associated with a proposed BMW 801 radial-engined layout that was tested experimentally. The Bf109J was the name tentatively given to a planned Spanish licence-built version of the Bf109G that was never built as such. The Bf109H was intended as a

Höhenjäger (high-altitude fighter) derivative that was not put into series production.

Various attempts were made to create a Bf109 successor, such as the Me209 (which began life to break the world speed record for landplanes, which it did in April 1939), and the Me309, but these did not enter series production. A Bf109F was used to try out the tricycle undercarriage layout that would have been employed for the Me309. Under the designation FiSk199, a Bf109G was modified to long-range fighter-bomber configuration with large long-range fuel tanks beneath the wings and a jettisonable tall tail wheel assembly to give clearance for the oversize under-wing stores – again this did not lead to a production configuration.

Much more successful was the Mistel (Mistletoe) composite programme. This involved a 'piggy-back' conversion with a Bf109 or Fw190 mounted on a framework above an explosives-filled Junkers Ju88 which would be flown by the pilot in the fighter, with the bomber released near to its target. This strange concept did see some operational use, principally using the Fw190 rather than the Bf109, although a Bf109 configuration attached to a DFS230 transport glider was also tried out.

Foreign employment and manufacture

The Bf109 was widely exported, and served with a number of countries which were aligned to the Nazi cause. These included Romania, Hungary (where there was also local assembly), Slovakia, Bulgaria and Italy. Some of these countries were privileged to receive versions of the Bf109 that were roughly contemporary with those being delivered to Luftwaffe units. Unfortunately for the Germans, virtually all these former allies eventually changed sides later in the Second World War, resulting in their Bf109s being used against the Germans – there were subsequently various occasions when Bf109s ended up fighting against each other in the same dog-fights. Yugoslavia was supplied with a number of Bf109Es in 1939, well before the German invasion in 1941, but some of these were delivered without weapons. A number of the survivors flew with pro-German Croatian forces later in the war, bolstered by supplies of later production Messerschmitts.

The country that probably made the best use of its Bf109s outside of Luftwaffe service was Finland. It defended itself admirably against Soviet aggression on two occasions while the Second World War raged, and employed a miscellany of aircraft types from all over the world. The Bf109G in particular proved to be highly successful against Soviet fighters and bombers in the Continuation War, and several Finnish pilots made impressive numbers of aerial victory claims.

The first export customer for the Bf109 was Switzerland. This country's armed forces had seen the potential of the Bf109 from the start, particularly after the excellent performance of the five early Bf109s that participated at the air meeting at Zürich-Dübendorf airfield in Switzerland between 23 July and 1 August 1937. Representations for the supply of Junkers Jumo-engine Bf109Ds were made soon after to the Germans, resulting in the supply of 10 Arado-built Bf109D-1s in December 1938 and January 1939. In early 1939 the Swiss followed this up with an order for 80 Bf109E-3. These aircraft, identified as Bf109E-3a (a for *ausland* or foreign), were all delivered from Messerschmitt Regensburg manufacture, and were fitted with Revi 3c A265 gunsights.

It was as well for the Swiss that these aircraft were in their inventory in the spring and early

BELOW: The Bf109 was widely exported, particularly though not exclusively to countries friendly to Nazi Germany. The first major export customer was neutral Switzerland. This Swiss Bf109E-3, serial number J-358, belly-landed in late 1944, showing that even by then the obsolete Bf109E was still of use to the Swiss. Swiss Bf109Es fought a brief and successful, but now largely forgotten, air war against German incursions into Swiss air space in 1940. *Peter Walter*

summer of 1940, when one of the forgotten incidents of the Second World War, a major air war between Germany and Switzerland, took place. German bombers en route to French targets deliberately violated neutral Swiss airspace, while numerous other violations occurred to test out the Swiss defences. The Swiss responded with considerable skill, shooting down around 66 Luftwaffe aircraft. This episode guaranteed Switzerland's freedom from German invasion during the war, and the Messerschmitts were fully involved in these engagements. The Swiss also built a small number of Bf109Es under licence, and received a batch of 12 Bf109Gs later in the war. These were supplied following the landing in Switzerland during April 1944 of a Luftwaffe Bf110G-4 night-fighter equipped with the latest SN-2 Lichtenstein radar.

The Germans were afraid that this new equipment would fall into Allied hands, and so paid Switzerland for the destruction of the aircraft in return for 12 new Bf109Gs, the first six from Regensburg manufacture and the final six with wooden tails, but fitted with Revi C/12D gunsights rather than the Revi 16b then being installed in Luftwaffe aircraft. The Swiss continued to operate Bf109s until after the Second World War, but a large number were taken out of service in 1946/7, with most being scrapped in 1948 and 1949. Total Swiss procurement of the Bf109 reached 114 examples – 10 Bf109D-1; 80 Bf109E-3; 8 Bf109E-3 licence-built; 2 Bf109F-4; 13 Bf109G-6 and 1 Bf109G-14.

Germany's Fascist partner Italy evaluated four Bf109Es in August 1939, but intended to make its own advanced fighter designs. However, in the spring of 1943 the Italians requested a number of combat aircraft, including 300 Bf109Gs, and a personal agreement between Hitler and Italian leader Mussolini ensured deliveries would be made in spite of the Luftwaffe needing all available aircraft. The first deliveries were made in April 1943, and by the time of the Italian armistice several months later Italy's Regia Aeronautica had received approximately 15 Bf109F-4s, and a variety of Gustavs, including 6 Bf109G-2s, 10 G-4s and 91 G-6s. Most of the Bf109Gs were new or relatively new, and were made by the Erla and Weiner-Neustadt factories within the large Bf109 manufacturing structure.

When the pro-German Italians continued the fight against the Allies after the September 1943 armistice, the newly created Aeronautica Nazionale Repubblicana (ANR) fought on the German side and received a large number of Bf109s, possibly totalling as many as 200 examples. Some of these were ex-Luftwaffe aircraft but others were totally up-to-date and included a number of Bf109Ks – again despite the Luftwaffe needing every available Bf109 that it could lay its hands on. Several of these Messerschmitts were still flyable at the end of the war, and proposals were made by the Italian company Agusta to recondition them for the newly reconstituted post-war Italian armed forces. Although this idea was initially attractive to the Italian authorities, eventually the survivors were scrapped as Italy began to receive large numbers of Allied combat types.

During the war, significant numbers of Bf109s fell into Allied hands. At the time, some of these captured aircraft were of great interest to Allied intelligence, especially if they represented a new mark of Bf109 that had not been examined by the Allies at close quarters before. Such was the case with Black 6, which was of considerable interest to the Allies, as it was probably at that time the best Bf109G-2 that had been captured. Some Bf109 examples like Black 6 were carefully evaluated subsequent to being captured. Other captured Bf109s, however, were used for less important tasks such as becoming unit 'hacks' for squadrons which made them flyable on newly-overrun airfields.

Large numbers of Bf109s were captured by the Allies at the end of the war. Many of these were in a poor state, either as a result of Allied bombing or strafing of factories and airfields, or as the result of ground crews deliberately destroying them. Some reasonably good examples were kept by the Allies for technical evaluation while the vast majority were simply scrapped. Small numbers of Bf109s were therefore retained by the US, Britain and the Soviet Union, but these were not of great importance at the end of the war – the Bf109 had by then become an obsolete design, and the victorious Allies had enough high-performance piston-engined fighters of their own. They were more interested in Germany's jet and rocket technology, and the Bf109 become little more than a curiosity.

Production of the Bf109 took place in two countries following the Second World War: Spain and Czechoslovakia. Both countries produced derivatives of the Bf109 that were somewhat different to the original Messerschmitt production layout of the Bf109, and a number of the Spanish-built examples are particularly important to the 'warbird' movement as they have formed the basis of some of the currently existing airworthy Bf109 lookalikes.

Spain

The Spanish manufacture of the Bf109 took place under the auspices of licence production, although this was something of a misnomer as the defeat of Germany in 1945 resulted in the suspension by the Allied powers in control of Germany of the production licences issued in the Nazi era.

The success of the Bf109 during the Spanish Civil War was very important. In helping to gain and retain air superiority for the Spanish Nationalist forces of General Franco, the Bf109 was highly significant in directly aiding the victory of Franco in 1939. During the fighting over Spain the Bf109 had shown itself to be an excellent warplane, no doubt much to the consternation of other nations in Europe and further afield. The Germans were well satisfied with their combat testing of the Bf109 and other weapons in the Spanish conflict, but

the Spanish were impressed too. A number of Bf109s stayed behind to form a significant nucleus of the rebuilt Spanish air force following Franco's victory, but the Spanish were keen to have more.

There already existed a flourishing aircraft industry in Spain, and although this had suffered during the civil war, it was still capable of building the Bf109. Nevertheless, to begin with the Spanish showed interest in resurrecting a French fighter design that had been in development just before the fall of France in June 1940. This was the Dewoitine D 520 which the Spanish intended to develop as the HS 50 with a Hispano-Suiza 12Z type 87 engine then under development. This idea was eventually abandoned, and in October 1942 the Spanish signed an agreement with Messerschmitt to produce under licence the Bf109G, specifically in its most advanced (at that time) G-6 version, and not the G-2 as sometimes claimed.

The Germans agreed to supply drawings, a complete airframe and 25 dismantled airframes, spares for the assembly of an additional 70 aircraft, and to oversee the start of production. The Spanish intended to manufacture a further 105 airframes on their own, making a total of 200 aircraft. These Spanish-assembled aircraft were tentatively designated Bf109J and were intended to be DB605A-powered. Hispano Aviación was chosen to be the prime contractor.

Unfortunately for the Spanish there were delays at once, and it was not until July 1943

BELOW: Following the victory of General Franco's fascist forces in the Spanish Civil War, a number of the former German-operated and German-supplied Bf109s that fought in the conflict were retained for the newly-formed Spanish air force under Franco's new regime. Included amongst them was this veteran Jumo-engined Bf109 which soldiered on into the later 1940s.
Philip Jarrett

that a pattern Bf109G-4/Trop was delivered,
with the 25 dismantled Bf109G-6 following
in October 1944, and some of these were
incomplete. The rest of the order never arrived,
and so the Spanish resorted to their own build
of an aircraft type on the lines of the Bf109G,
the licence agreement originally signed with
Messerschmitt by then having been rendered
null and void by the Allied occupying powers.
Without DB605A engines, however, the Spanish
subsequently reverted to the Hispano-Suiza 12Z
87-series engine originally envisaged for the HS
50 project.

Various test flights were eventually made
with the HS 12Z 87-series engine installed in a
suitably-modified airframe from among those
earlier supplied. This opened the way for over
20 of the 25 previously-supplied airframes to
be finished and flown with the Hispano-Suiza
powerplant under the designation HA-1109-
J1L. In July 1946 Hispano was contracted to
build 200 new fighters along these lines, but
problems with the HS 12Z 87 engine installation
resulted in new airframes being finished without
engines. Subsequently the more advanced
HS 12Z 17-series engine was bought from
the French Hispano-Suiza company, resulting
in some of the completed airframes being
powered by this engine and called HA-1109-

K1L. As many as 65 may have been so built,
with the first flight taking place in May 1951.

Salvation for the Spanish connection came
with the agreement between the Spanish
authorities and Rolls-Royce in Britain to
supply Merlin 500-series engines to power the
Spanish-produced airframes. The 500-series
Merlin had been designed for civil airliner use,
and there were surplus engines available. The
resulting Hispano concoction of Spanish-
built airframe and British engine created the
aircraft type that we are all now familiar with,
the HA-1112-M1L, military designation C.4K,
but better known as the Buchón. This name in
Spanish means a bird with a big pouch, chest
or belly, which is very appropriate because the
installation of the comparatively large Merlin in
the small former Messerschmitt airframe gave
an ungainly chin or pot-bellied appearance.
The Spanish who flew them and worked on
them usually called them 'Messer'. The first
flight was made in late 1954, and between then
and the late 1950s, 169 production single-seat
examples were completed, plus two two-seater
HA-1112-M4L. Armament comprised two
20mm Hispano-Suiza 404/408 cannons (one in
each wing) and Oerlikon or Pilatus 80mm rocket
sets beneath the wings.

The Buchóns had a short service life, but

some saw action as ground-attack aircraft with the Spanish air force in the Spanish Sahara where fighting took place in the late 1950s and early 1960s. A considerable number of them were airworthy in the mid-1960s when the Spanish began to look for more modern alternatives. The type was officially retired in late 1965, although some appear to have remained on the books of the Spanish air force into 1967. At that time the 'warbird' movement was starting to become important, and thankfully many of the soon-to-be surplus Buchóns were sold to private individuals or film companies. Some have subsequently masqueraded in several movies as Bf109s, but the type instantly became famous, and gained immortal fame, for its role in the motion picture *Battle of Britain* – in which the Luftwaffe fighter arm was solely represented by these Bf109 lookalikes, albeit with their prominent Merlin powerplant installation giving the game away as to their origins.

Czechoslovakia

During the latter stages of the Second World War Bf109s were assembled in the Protectorate of Bohemia and Moravia – the German name for the dismembered part of Czechoslovakia that was left after the Munich Agreement and which had subsequently been taken over by the Germans in 1939. This included the underground Diana Werke in unfinished railway tunnels near Tišnov. Following the reunification of Czechoslovakia in May 1945 these manufacturing facilities were still in place, and a large number of part-completed airframes and engines were available for possible future use, together with drawings and tooling.

The newly-reconstituted Czech Air Force was in need of re-equipment, having a mixed-bag of donated former RAF and Soviet types (Czech airmen fought with both the RAF and the Soviet Union against the Germans during the war). A possible solution to bolster the mixed-bag of ex-RAF Spitfires and Soviet-produced Lavochkin fighters that were immediately available was to restart manufacture of the Bf109. To that end the revitalised Avia company at Prague-Čakovice began to assemble Bf109G lookalikes with DB605A or D engines, called the C-10 (later military designation S-99) for single-seaters and C-110 (later military CS-99) for the two-seaters. The latter approximated to the wartime two-seater Bf109G-12. The first of these flew in February 1946. Altogether 21 (possibly 23) S-99 and 29 CS-99 were completed, although the Czechs technically did not hold a licence to produce them – however,

ABOVE: Looking very elegant in its dull metal grey and red finish, this Bf109G look-alike is a Czechoslovak-built, post-war Avia S-99. About twenty-three of these unlicensed Bf109G copies were made in Czechoslovakia, with DB605A or D engines – the supply of which was very limited. The aircraft was registered OK-BYH and was operated by the Czechoslovak LH SNB (Letecká hlídka Sboru národní bezpečnosti, or 'Police Air Patrol').
4+ Publishing Co

ABOVE: The Avia S-199 was the Czechoslovakian post-war derivative of the Bf109G, powered by a Junkers Jumo 211 (M-211) bomber engine. This example was part of a 'private' collection of former Czech-operated military aircraft before it was scrapped. *4+ Publishing Co*

BELOW: The Avia S-199 was a beast to fly, but served in numbers with the Czechoslovakian air force into the mid-1950s until replaced by jet fighters. The type had a unique rearwards-sliding cockpit canopy. *Jaroslav Matoulek Collection via 4+ Publishing Co*

as all German licences had been suspended by the Allied occupying powers, this was not a problem. Then fate intervened and a warehouse fire destroyed many of the remaining usable DB605 engines. Avia began a search for a suitable replacement power plant. Unfortunately, the only engine type that was readily available was the Junkers Jumo 211, a bomber engine that owed some connection to the Jumo 210 that powered the original Bf109B, C and D series. Undaunted, Avia redesigned the Bf109 to take the larger, heavier and less responsive Jumo 211, the result being a distinctively ugly front end that did nothing for the Bf109's flying characteristics or centre of gravity. The Jumo 211 (M-211 in Czechoslovakia) was not a suitable fighter engine, having too much torque and rotating in the opposite direction to the DB605. Originally, in order to help counter the DB605's torque, the Bf109's vertical tailplane had been made specially curved on one side, and this needed to be reversed due to the opposite rotation of the Jumo 211. As a result of this re-engining, Avia created a beast, which had all the bad habits of the Bf109 on take-off and landing, but magnified several times and with poor handling now also included.

LEFT: The Avia CS-199 was the two-seat stablemate of the single-seat S-199 fighter, both types being Jumo 211 (M-211)-powered. This is the only known surviving example, c/n 565, which is on display at the Letecké Muzeum (Aviation Museum) at Prague-Kbely in the Czech Republic. *Malcolm V. Lowe*

BELOW: Although the canopy of very early-production two-seat Avia CS-199s was similar to the wartime Bf109G-12, later production CS-199s used the rearwards/forwards-sliding canopy type seen here on the Prague-Kbely example, based on that of the Avia C-2 (Czech-built Arado Ar96). *Malcolm V. Lowe*

Known to Avia as the C-210, up to 543 single-seaters with the Jumo 211F (M-211F) engine were built by Avia and Aero, with the Czech military designation S-199. The first example flew in April 1947, and production continued until 1951. These aircraft were disliked by their pilots, and gained the nickname 'Mezek' (mule) – and other names too. Nevertheless, the type served with the Czech Air Force in front-line units into the mid-1950s when they were replaced by locally-produced MiG-15 jet fighters. One good point of the S-199 was its one-piece clear-view rearwards-sliding cockpit canopy, which was an improvement over the wartime Messerschmitt canopy arrangements. Armament comprised two MG131 13mm machine guns in the upper forward fuselage, and an MG151/20 20mm cannon in a 'gondola' under each wing. A 250kg bomb could be carried beneath the fuselage, or a 300-litre drop tank. A two-seater derivative, the CS-199, was also built, which first flew in January 1949.

Approximately 82 were constructed, some from re-manufactured CS-99s. The two-seater CS-199 used a completely different cockpit canopy arrangement compared to the German-built Bf109G-12, and had both opening sections manufactured to slide rather than being hinged to the side. Israel purchased 25 examples of the S-199, and at least 23 of these reached the country from May 1948 and went into action straight away during the Israeli war of independence. Most, if not all, had been withdrawn by the end of that year as the Israelis obtained more reliable and easier to operate aircraft types.

Bf109 facts and figures

Technical specifications

The following are representative specifications from official German documentation for three different marks of Bf109. It is interesting to note the increase in available engine power from the early Bf109B to the later Bf109G, but also the alarming rise in take-off weights. Although the Bf109G-6 had a theoretical maximum speed that was higher than that of its predecessors, in practice and in combat configuration it was slower, particularly when weighed down with the underwing 'gondolas' for MG151/20 cannons. The latter were necessary to give the Bf109G extra 'punch', especially when trying to combat US daylight bombers high over Germany, but in practice these bulky add-ons made the Messerschmitt slower and more vulnerable to the US escort fighters which were increasingly numerous and of higher performance as the war progressed. Although the specifications quoted for the Bf109G are specific to the G-6, they are also representative for the mark of Black 6, which was a Bf109G-2.

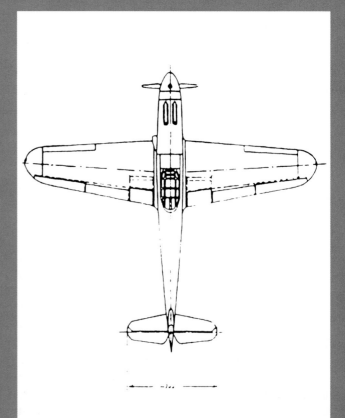

Taken from the official manual for the Bf109G-6/U4, D.(Luft) T.2109 G-6/U4, dated 22 February 1944, this general arrangement drawing confirms the dimensions for the Bf109G-6, which are also correct for earlier Bf109G versions, including the Bf109G-2, Black 6. *Messerschmitt AG/Malcolm V. Lowe*

Messerschmitt Bf109B-1

Wingspan	32ft 4.5in (9.87m)
Length	28ft 0.66in (8.55m)
Maximum speed	292mph (470kmh) at 14,764ft (4,500m)
Service ceiling	29,528ft (9,000m)
Range	404 miles (650km)
Armament	Two 7.92mm machine guns in upper forward fuselage
Engine	One Junkers Jumo 210D inline piston engine, of 680hp
Crew	One

Messerschmitt Bf109E-3

Wingspan	32ft 4.5in (9.87m)
Length	28ft 4.5in (8.65m) (or 8.76m sometimes quoted)
Maximum speed	354mph (570 kmh) at 12,303ft (3,750m)
Maximum take-off weight	5,875lb (2,665kg)
Range	Approximately 413 miles (665km)
Service ceiling	36,090ft (11,000m)
Armament	Two 7.92mm machine guns in upper forward fuselage, two wing-mounted 20mm cannons
Engine	One Daimler-Benz DB601A inline piston engine, of 1,100hp
Crew	One

Messerschmitt Bf109G-6

Wingspan	32ft 6.7in (9.924m)
Length	29ft 4in (8.94m)
Maximum speed	386mph (621kmh) at 22,638ft (6,900m)
Maximum take-off weight	6,944lb (3,150kg)
Range	Approximately 621 miles (1,000km) (with drop tank)
Service ceiling	37,894ft (11,550m)
Armament	One 20mm cannon 'engine-mounted', two 13mm machine guns in upper forward fuselage
Engine	One Daimler-Benz DB605A inline piston engine, of 1,475hp
Crew	One

Bf109 weaponry

The Bf109 was a well-armed warplane, and reflected the evolving German military thinking of the Second World War era in terms of fighter aircraft armament, that heavy-calibre weapons in comparatively small numbers were preferable to the British concept of the later 1930s of multiple rifle-calibre machine guns. The British eventually modified this idea to include heavier calibre weapons, while the Bf109 was developed in time into a formidable fighter and ground-attack aircraft – although the addition of some weapon systems adversely affected performance. Indeed, throughout its life the Bf109 underwent considerable up-gunning and weapons evolution, particularly to suit operational requirements.

The original armament fitted to the initial Bf109B production model comprised two 7.92mm Rheinmetall-Borsig MG17 machine guns, mounted in the forward upper fuselage ahead of the cockpit and synchronised to fire through the propeller arc. There had been the intention to mount a third MG17 centrally, in the engine compartment to fire through the propeller hub (the so-called 'engine-mounted' installation), but this was found to be impracticable even though the Jumo 210 engine could be configured to allow this. Each gun had 500 rounds, but in later models this was extended to 1,000rpg. In the Bf109C the armament was uprated, partly as a result of operational experience with the Bf109B,

to include a further MG17 in each wing, outboard of the propeller arc and therefore not needing to be synchronised, in addition to the established two MG17 in the forward upper fuselage. The wing guns had 420 rounds each. It was intended that a centrally-mounted, Oerlikon-licence MG FF 20mm cannon would be installed, but again attempts to perfect this 'engine-mounted' installation were not successful due to vibration and other issues and the weapon was not included on production aircraft. This armament arrangement stayed the same for the Bf109D, the last of the Jumo-engine Bf109 versions.

The MG17 was an air-cooled machine gun with electric firing and pneumatic charging – the compressed air bottles for which were located in the fuselage, although on some later models of the Bf109 these were moved to the wings. The upper forward fuselage installation involved the two guns being staggered due to the positioning of the ammunition chutes, with the left-hand weapon slightly ahead of the right-hand one. The MG17 had a rate of fire, in its best optimum operating conditions, of 1,200 rounds per minute, although as with most airborne weapons the operating altitude, outside temperature and other related features could reduce this rate of fire.

This basic weapons configuration, of two upper forward fuselage and two wing-mounted MG17 was carried on into the first of the Daimler-Benz-powered Bf109E production examples, in the Bf109E-1 block. However, the

BELOW: Diagram from an early Bf109E manual showing the wing structure of that version, and the installation within the wing of the 7.92mm MG17 machine gun. The Bf109 was not designed to carry internal wing armament, and the installation of these weapons within the wings from the Bf109C onwards necessitated modification to the main spar and wing structure. Later Bf109 production versions, including the Bf109F and Bf109G, did not carry internal wing armament. This was in contrast to the Focke-Wulf Fw190, which partnered the Bf109 from 1941 onwards as the Luftwaffe's main fighter types, which was designed from the first to carry machine guns and cannons within its wings. *Malcolm V. Lowe Collection*

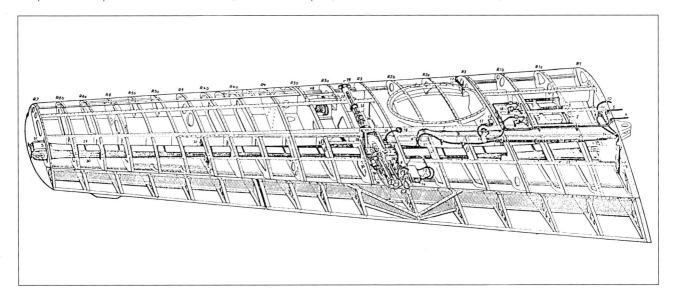

ABOVE: The weapons installation in the upper forward fuselage of the captured Bf109E-4 flown by Franz von Werra. In particular the staggered installation of the two 7.92mm MG17 machine guns can be seen. The left-hand gun is slightly further forward due to the ammunition feed arrangement. *Philip Jarrett*

RIGHT: The ubiquitous Mauser MG151/20 20mm cannon was standardised in the central 'engine-mounted' location in the Bf109 from the Bf109F-4 onwards. It would have been fitted to Black 6 in that location. This excellent and widely-used 20mm cannon was also carried by some later Bf109s in under-wing 'gondolas' in the R6 add-on configuration. *Jozef And'al*

Bf109E-3 introduced a much heavier armament. Although the two MG17 machine guns in the upper forward fuselage were retained for the E-3, the wing-mounted MG17s were deleted and were replaced by an MG FF 20mm cannon, one in each wing. This was a much larger and heavier weapon than the MG17, and it was mounted slightly further outboard than the MG17; a prominent bulge on the wing lower surface was introduced so that the cannon and its associated 60-round drum magazine could be accommodated within the Emil's wing, which had not really been intended to house such a bulky weapon (indeed, the Bf109's wing had not been designed with the carriage of weapons, internal or external, as a primary consideration).

At that time the MG FF was already becoming obsolete, and it had a slow rate of fire of 530 rounds per minute. It did however represent a significant up-gunning of the Bf109. It was also fitted in the wing of the Bf109E-4 and E-7 versions, in a configuration identical to the Bf109E-3. There is also documented and photographic evidence to suggest that some Bf109C-3 also had this wing cannon arrangement. An attempt was additionally made to centrally locate this weapon in the so-called 'engine-mounted' position for the Emil series,

and the Bf109E-2 and some E-3 apparently had this configuration although in small numbers. A development of the MG FF, the MG FF/M which fired slightly different types of cannon shells, was made available for use in the Bf109 and there is evidence that it was fitted instead of the standard MG FF in some aircraft.

In line with the expanding roles envisaged for the Bf109 as the Second World War developed, several marks of the Bf109E were configured specifically for fighter-bomber operations, with a weapons carrier attached beneath the fuselage for the carriage of bombs. Some examples of the earlier Emil versions were so fitted, and the concept was further expanded with the E-7 which was able to mount various weapons carriers beneath the fuselage centreline such as the ETC 50 or ETC 250 bomb racks, the number of the carrier referring to the size of bomb(s) in kilograms that it could mount (4x50kg or 1x250kg). These weapons carriers were electrically activated, but also had an emergency mechanical release option. All fighter-bomber Bf109s carried their bombs beneath the fuselage, unlike the Spitfire which could carry bombs beneath its wings – again underlining the fact that the Spitfire's wing was stronger and had been envisaged from the beginning for the provision of various weapons combinations, which the Bf109's had not.

The radical makeover that was given to the Bf109 series with the introduction of the Bf109F resulted in some alterations to the weapons provision. From the Bf109F-2, a successful centrally-located cannon installation in the so-called 'engine-mounted' position firing through the propeller spinner was introduced. The weapon used for this installation was the Mauser MG151/15 15mm cannon, which proved to be a satisfactory set-up and paved the way for subsequent Bf109 versions to have the centrally-mounted cannon as standard – although there is evidence that some at least of the Bf109F-1 series were fitted with an

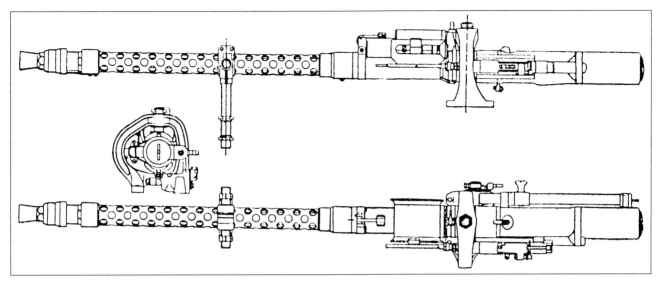

MG FF 20mm cannon in that central location. Otherwise, the Bf109F series saw the upper forward fuselage MG17 installation retained from the Bf109E and earlier series.

From the Bf109F-4 version onwards, the centrally-mounted cannon armament was standardised on the MG151/20 20mm cannon (both the MG151/15 and MG151/20 were from the same design layout, but with different barrels and size of ammunition). Also for the Bf109F series, there were various fighter-bomber variations with provision for under-fuselage bomb attachment, the Bf109F-4/B fighter-bomber being particularly widely used with a number of possible bomb combinations. The Bf109F series also became a part of the widescale introduction by the Luftwaffe of special Rüstsatz conversion kits or sets (often concerned with add-on armament options) for installation in the field. Significant among these was the R7 option, for an underwing fairing or 'gondola' under each wing in which an MG151/20 was mounted, thus considerably adding to the Bf109's growing firepower, although these drag-inducing installations reduced performance.

The Bf109F-4/R7 has sometimes been viewed as the ultimate Bf109 fighter version. The Bf109G series that followed from the Bf109F continued the armament layout established with the Bf109F-4, again with Rüstsatz options. By then the Rüstsatz alternative in which an MG151/20 was installed beneath each wing in an underwing fairing or 'gondola' was called the R6, and the fitments

for these fairings were built-in on the production line. A different planned installation, mounting a Rheinmetall-Borsig MK108 30mm cannon in an underwing fairing under each wing was considered as the U5 modification. Therefore Black 6, which was a standard Bf109G-2, mounted two MG17 7.92mm machine guns in the upper forward fuselage, and a centrally-mounted MG151/20 20mm cannon firing through its propeller spinner. The fact that it was a Bf109G-2/Trop did not affect the type of armament fitted.

Later in the Bf109G series production, a major change was made with the deletion of the MG17 7.92mm machine guns in the upper forward fuselage location and their replacement with two harder-hitting MG131 13mm machine guns. These fast-firing weapons (900 rounds per minute) were a major upgrading of the Bf109's capability and were introduced from the Bf109G-5 version onwards. They would normally have had 300rpg in a typical installation. This gave versions such as the Bf109G-6/R-6 a considerable array of weaponry with which to combat US bomber formations over Germany from later in 1943 onwards to augment increasingly stretched Fw190 units, but the up-gunning came at a price in increased heaviness and drag. The installation of the two MG131s in the upper forward fuselage necessitated the fitting of a prominent bulge to each side of the engine cowling ahead of the cockpit to accommodate the two weapons with their larger breech blocks and ammunition feed chutes side-by-side, further adding to the

ABOVE: An official manufacturer's drawing from 1940 showing the general arrangement of the 7.92mm MG17 machine gun as fitted in the upper forward fuselage (one on each side of the centreline) of all production Bf109s up to the Bf109G-5 and G-6 series onwards. This is therefore the weapon type that was fitted in that position on the Bf109G-2, Black 6. *Messerschmitt AG/ Malcolm V. Lowe*

ever-growing number of bumps and protrusions that were giving a detrimental effect to overall performance. Some Bf109G-6, however, were fitted with the Daimler-Benz DB605AS engine rather than the standard DB605A of the Bf109G-6, the 'AS' installation resulting in a more streamlined cowling shape that did away with the prominent bulges ahead of the cockpit.

A number of Bf109G-6 were fitted with an MK108 30mm cannon in the centrally-located so-called 'engine-mounted' position firing through the propeller spinner in the Bf109G-6/U4 configuration, in replacement of the MG151/20 usually located there by that phase in Bf109 production. This very destructive weapon was potentially ideal for anti-bomber operations, but had a slow rate of fire (600 rounds per minute, but only 60 rounds could be carried in that location) and was prone to jamming. It was also fitted to the following Bf109G production versions which went after the G-6, namely the Bf109G-14 and the Bf109G-10. Both these versions had the MG131 13mm machine gun installation in the upper forward fuselage, and some had 'AS' engines in which the two prominent cowling bulges were replaced with the more streamlined cowling shape associated with that particular engine installation.

The by then often used Rüstsatz conversion kits were available for use on many of these late-production Bf109 versions. The final major production series of the Bf109, the Bf109K and particularly the Bf109K-4, also had the MK108 30mm cannon for the centrally-located so-called 'engine-mounted' position, plus the usual pair of MG131 13mm machine guns in the upper forward fuselage.

As the air fighting against American bomber formations high over Germany became more intense in the latter stages of the war, so the Germans tried out a number of innovations to attempt to counter these ever more frequent and successful raids. An important underwing store used against formations of heavy bombers was the 21cm WGr 21 mortar rocket or 21cm Sondergerät, which was a tube-mounted one-round rocket intended for use against large formations of enemy bombers where its blast effect could be destructive to one or more aircraft. It was, however, notoriously difficult to aim and its use in combat was limited. In the case of the Bf109, one of these jettisonable contraptions could be mounted below each wing. The drag that was produced further degraded the aircraft's performance, and also compromised its manoeuvrability, making the Bf109s carrying this weapons system even easier for US escort fighters to combat.

Weapon aiming in the Bf109 was by means of a reflector gunsight. This type of equipment was known to the Germans as Reflexvisier or Revi gunsight. In the initial production Bf109B the type installed was a rudimentary Revi 3, and this type was also fitted to some examples of the later Jumo 210-engined Bf109s as well as some Bf109E versions. However, it was superseded by the excellent and very simple to operate Revi C/12 series, which was widely used on most early to mid-production Bf109s. These gunsights had no computing capacity but were much preferred by Luftwaffe pilots to the original Revi 3. Nevertheless, some Bf109s retained a rudimentary ring and bead type sight in addition to the gunsight. The Revi C/12 came in two versions, the Revi C/12 C for simple gun/cannon sighting in aerial combat, and the Revi C/12 D for multiple weapon use including bomb aiming for fighter-bomber operations.

In 1943 a new gunsight was gradually introduced, the Revi 16b, which was a more advanced but nevertheless reliable and still comparatively simple weapons aiming sight. This device was used during early Bf109G manufacture, and in the Bf109K version. Later

BELOW: The hard-hitting 30mm Rheinmetall-Borsig MK108 cannon was potentially one of the most destructive weapons fitted to German fighters during Second World War. A large, heavy and bulky weapon, it had a comparatively slow rate of fire. It was intended for later versions of the Bf109, either in the engine-mounted location to fire centrally through the propeller spinner, or in under-wing gondolas. The engine-mounted location was used particularly for later marks of the Bf109G and K. *Peter Walter*

in the war a completely new and advanced gunsight became available. This was the EZ 42 gyroscopic gunsight, a sophisticated (for its time) piece of equipment which would have made deflection shooting an easier function and was more on a par with the excellent K-14A computing gunsight used in late-war US fighters such as the later production versions of the North American P-51 Mustang. Although intended for use in the Bf109K it was not adopted, due in part to the disintegrating wartime situation in Germany and because it was too bulky for the cramped confines of the Bf109 cockpit. The type of gunsight fitted to Black 6 was, as far as is known, a Revi C/12 D, and that type is now installed in the aircraft for display purposes in its location at the RAF Museum, Hendon.

A number of innovations were tried out for the Bf109 on a more unit-level or even individual level to aid in fighting enemy aircraft. Among the best-known of these were the experiments

ABOVE: A line-up of 21cm WGr21 mortar rocket-equipped Bf109G-6/R2 fighters. Fitted with one of these one-round unguided rocket devices beneath each wing, the Bf109 was intended to break up formations of high-flying US heavy bombers, by lobbing the projectiles in the general direction of a B-17 Flying Fortress or B-24 Liberator bomber formation, the blast theoretically bringing down one or more of the bombers and scattering others. In practice the weapon proved difficult to aim precisely, and the Messerschmitts carrying these cumbersome devices were easy prey for defending US escort fighters. *Philip Jarrett*

carried out for the famed German fighter pilot Adolf Galland, who had three Bf109Fs specially converted. They were fitted with various modifications to increase their armament, including one which had MG FF wing cannons – he considered the Bf109F in its basic production configuration to be too lightly-armed to be truly effective. Galland also used a special telescope/telescopic sight, pointing through the windscreen, to identify aircraft at long range while in the air.

ABOVE: The two highest-scoring fighter pilots of all time. On the left is Erich Hartmann (with 352 'kills'), and Gerhard Barkhorn, with 301 aerial victories.
Malcolm V. Lowe Collection

Bf109 Fighter aces

During its comparatively long service life, the Bf109 was flown by many of Germany's most successful and best-known pilots. A significant proportion of these pilots became aces, and some racked up impressive scores of aerial victories in the Bf109. The German method of scoring aerial victories in the Second World War was straightforward (unlike that of some other countries), with official ace status being granted to any pilot who achieved five or more aerial kills. There has been considerable debate among historians about the authenticity of some of these scores, particularly when German claims for particular days or even specific actions and combats do not tally with known losses of Allied aircraft. To cloud the picture further, the German bureaucratic process for assessing the claims broke down in the opening weeks of 1945 as the situation in the country worsened, making many claims in the final stages of the war impossible to verify, unless they can be accurately cross-referenced against known Allied losses.

Nevertheless, there is no doubt that many pilots achieved remarkable successes while piloting the Bf109. The type was flown by the three top-scoring fighter aces of the Second World War, all of whom were Luftwaffe pilots: Erich Hartmann, the world's highest scoring fighter pilot, claiming 352 victories; Gerhard Barkhorn claiming 301 victories; and Günther Rall claiming 275 victories. They flew with Luftwaffe fighter wing JG52, a unit which was credited with the staggering total of over 10,000 victories, chiefly on the Eastern Front – although it must again be stressed that the verification of at least some of these is questionable. Erich Hartmann was a true enthusiast for the Bf109 and chose to fly the type despite being eligible to pilot other warplanes such as the much-vaunted Focke-Wulf Fw190. Similarly, Hans-Joachim Marseille, the highest scoring German ace in North Africa, also claimed all of his 158 victories while flying the Bf109.

In its widespread service with countries other than Germany, the Bf109 was also used to good effect by non-German pilots. These included the Romanian ace Alexandru Serbănescu with 47 victories, the Hungarian Szentgyörgyi Dezsó with 34 victories, the Croatian Mato Dukovac with 44 victories, and the Finnish Ilmari Juutilainen with 94 victories – the latter being the highest scoring non-German fighter pilot in the Second World War and its associated conflicts. Again, not all these victories can be easily verified, and some are the result of a somewhat unusual system (like that of the Romanians) of allocating aerial kills.

Without doubt the Bf109 has been credited with more aerial victories than any other

BELOW: Germany's best-known fighter pilot from the Second World War was Adolf Galland. He flew the Bf109 in combat but had a rather love-hate relationship with the type, feeling that some versions were under-gunned. Galland is on the right, with Reichsmarschall Hermann Göring (centre).
Peter Walter

aircraft. At the present count, no less than 105 Bf109 pilots, and possibly four others, were acknowledged by the German claims verification service with the destruction of 100 or more enemy aircraft. Among these, 13 achieved more than 200 kills, and two of them (Hartmann and Barkhorn) scored more than 300. It is a sobering thought that between them, these particular Luftwaffe pilots were credited with nearly 15,000 kills. Across the board, ace status was bestowed to more than 2,500 Luftwaffe pilots, although some of these achieved aerial victories in more than one type – with several racking up impressive scores in the Fw190.

The majority of Bf109 pilots made their aerial victories in combat with Soviet forces, particularly in the aerial battles that followed Operation Barbarossa in 1941 when vast numbers of antiquated and obsolete Soviet aircraft were destroyed. At that time the Fw190 had not yet entered service, and the meticulous Luftwaffe records state that during Operation Barbarossa German Bf109 pilots of the seven fighter wings involved – JG3, JG27, JG51, JG53, JG54, JG77 and LG2 – claimed 7,355 aerial victories. At the same time, there were 350 Bf109 losses confirmed in aerial combat. This gave a ratio of just over 21:1, which is arguably the greatest kill to loss ratio ever recorded in aerial combat for which reliable figures exist. It was not just the Germans who achieved impressive numbers of aerial victories with the Bf109: Finnish pilots made claims for 667 aerial victories with the type, during their conflict with the Soviet Union. Based on these figures, the Bf109 was a highly effective and successful fighter and even later in the war the type could still hold its own when flown by a skilled pilot, despite being past its best from the Bf109G model onwards. Unfortunately for the Germans, skilled and experienced pilots were increasingly at a premium as the war progressed, with many top fighter pilots being lost as US, British, Commonwealth and Soviet airmen gained the upper hand.

Combat comparisons

The Bf109 was of advanced design and construction when it first appeared in production form in 1937, and was a fine performer particularly in its earlier versions before the weight and aerodynamics began to suffer from the Bf109G onwards. During the Second World War many trials were performed on captured Bf109s by the British to get under the skin of the erstwhile and successful adversary of RAF Spitfires and Hurricanes (and everything else in the RAF's inventory). Some of these trials were flown against Allied combat aircraft and the German Focke-Wulf Fw190, and their conclusions are revealing (Black 6 was a participant in some of the studies).

Conducted by the Air Fighting Development Unit at RAF Wittering, a captured Bf109G was compared with the North American P-51 Mustang in its Packard Merlin-powered Mustang Mk.III version (P-51B/C equivalent), the actual aircraft used being a late-production Mustang Mk.III. The AFDU report was dated 8 March 1944, and sung the praises of the Mustang in comparison to the Bf109G. Regarding the Bf109, it was found that the altitude for maximum performance from the Bf109G's Daimler-Benz DB605A engine was 16,000ft (4,877m) – this is known as the rated altitude of the aircraft – but at that height the Mustang was 30mph (48kmh) faster in level flight. The Mustang was also faster, by 50mph (80kmh) at 30,000ft (9,144m). Like several other Axis fighters, the Bf109 had a slightly better rate of climb up to some 20,000ft (6,096m), but from there upwards the Mustang gained a slight advantage. When 'zoom climbed' (employing speed obtained in a dive to increase the speed of climb) there was no noticeable difference in their respective rates. In a dive the Mustang Mk.III could draw steadily away from the Bf109G. In turning manoeuvres the Mustang could out-turn the Bf109, but there was little to choose between them in rate of roll. The firepower of the Messerschmitt was noted as being potentially much heavier than the Mustang, with two 13mm machine guns and three 20mm cannon (although operationally the Bf109G would need under-wing 'gondolas' to mount the additional two 20-mm cannons, in the Rüstsatz 6 add-on modification, thus slightly impairing overall performance), but the German fighter had nothing like the Mustang's endurance, showing only some 90 minutes under combat conditions – a paltry amount compared to the long-legged Mustang. The Bf109's cockpit was noted as being far more cramped, and its pilot also had a comparatively restricted view from the cockpit.

In the trials made with the Fw190A, which was perhaps the most formidable of German fighters in the mid to late-war period, the Mustang was found to be nearly 50mph (80kmh) faster up to 28,000ft (8,534m), which increased to an excellent 70mph (113kmh) above that height. Little overall difference was found in rate of climb, but there was a slight advantage for the Mustang in turns. The German fighter had a vastly superior rate of roll, but the Fw190 was capably out-dived by the Mustang. Overall the Mustang came out very well from these comparative trials, against both the main German fighters, which was an important indicator of how the air war would develop as 1944 progressed – a year in which the US Army Air Force's Mustangs eventually reigned supreme in the skies over Germany, having wrested air superiority comprehensively from the Luftwaffe.

Trials were similarly performed with the Bf109G flying against several British types, including the recent and formidable Rolls-Royce Griffon-powered Spitfire Mk.XIV, which entered service in February 1944. The Spitfire proved to be 25mph (40kmh) faster than the Bf109G up to 16,000ft (4,877m), which was the rated altitude of the Bf109G, at which height the Spitfire was only 10mph (16kmh) faster, but higher than that the Spitfire drew away, so as to be a very useful 50mph (80kmh) faster at 30,000ft (9,144m). At the Bf109G's rated altitude the climb performance of the two was roughly the same, but at all other altitudes the Spitfire's climb performance was superior. Indeed, climbing at full throttle the Spitfire easily out-climbed the Messerschmitt. In a dive the Bf109G had a slight initial gain, but this was lost when speeds reached and exceeded 380mph (612kmh). When 'zoom climbed' the Spitfire easily pulled away from the Messerschmitt. The Spitfire was also found to be able to easily out-turn the Messerschmitt, and to have a

better rate of roll. This was all bad news for the Luftwaffe pilots flying the Bf109G, who would increasingly face the Spitfire Mk.XIV as 1944 wore on.

Some trials were also flown between the Bf109G and a Spitfire LF Mk.IX, a type which was still very prominent in the RAF's inventory at that time. Again it was not good news for the Bf109G. This mark of Spitfire, which had entered service in mid-1942 and which at once had started to redress the balance in air combat between the Spitfire and Bf109, had a speed advantage at all heights, except just above the Bf109G's rated altitude. It also climbed faster, including in the 'zoom climb' manoeuvre, but was slower in a dive. Nevertheless it had a superior turning circle and roll rate.

As can be seen from these comparisons, the Bf109G did not come out particularly well against a range of important Allied warplanes. This reinforces the view of some Luftwaffe pilots at the time, and of writers since, that the Bf109 series had passed its best with the Bf109G, which was heavier and slower than its immediate Bf109 marks, and yet had to face increasingly higher-performance Allied fighters.

Pilot's comments

In comparing the Bf109G to the Spitfire it is useful to examine the thoughts of a pilot who has flown both types. Dave Southwood is an ex-RAF Empire Test Pilots' School pilot, and has flown all manner of aircraft, both modern and historic. He was, therefore, an excellent candidate for piloting Black 6 during the period when it was airworthy. Here, he compares some aspects of the Spitfire (of several different marks) and the Bf109G.

Pilot comfort

The Spitfire has rudder pedals and seat height that are easy to adjust once in the cockpit. I am 6ft 3in (1.90m) tall and find that the Spitfire has plenty of room and is quite comfortable. In the Bf109, the rudder pedals and seat height have to be adjusted by the ground crew before the pilot gets into the cockpit, and it is not quick and easy to do. The cockpit is cramped and you need to sit with your head as close to the top of the canopy as possible in order to get the best possible forward view. Thus, the space for head movement is much less than the Spitfire. On this aspect, the Spitfire wins hands down!

Field of view (FOV)

The Spitfire on the ground has an area of obscuration ahead due to the long nose that is common with all Second World War tail wheel fighters. In flight, the forward, upward and lateral FOV are quite good, although the high fuselage back restricts rearwards FOV significantly; hence the introduction of the 'low back' versions as an operational requirement to improve rearwards FOV. The 109 FOV is similar on the ground, but with the tropical air filter fitted to the supercharger intake (on the left of the nose like 'Black 6') it is much worse. In flight the limited head room and framed canopy make the overall FOV worse than the Spitfire, and rearwards FOV is worse due to the linear nature of the canopy. The Spitfire is somewhat better on this one.

Handling qualities

How long have you got? I will try to simplify this, and will add the caveat that I have not taken either aircraft to the extremes of speed, altitude or g to which they would have been flown in combat due to the need to conserve airframe and engine life. Therefore, I cannot really comment on absolute performance figures.

Ground handling

The Achilles heel of the Spitfire is that it is very 'tail light'. If you brake a little harshly whilst taxiing or during landing, you will tip it on its nose in a heartbeat. During landing, I consider the brakes firstly to be a control for keeping straight by differential use and only secondarily to slow you down. Likewise, excessive power during engine run-ups or taxiing in a tail wind will raise the tail and often result in striking the prop on the ground. The 109 is tail heavy and does not suffer from this problem although the narrow track undercarriage does make tight turns difficult on wet grass as the inner wheel will lock and the aircraft just slides straight on. One additional consideration is that engine cooling for both types is similarly poor on the ground, and the coolant will boil in around 5–12 minutes depending on the coolant temperature at engine start and ambient air temperature.

Take-off

The Spitfire has lots of aileron and rudder power, and control is reasonably straightforward although if you raise the tail too high you will strike the propeller on the ground. The Bf109 is challenging, to say the least, as it is markedly directionally unstable (massive over steer in car terms). If you increase power too rapidly or raise the tail too quickly you do not have the rudder power to counter the resulting yaw and a 'ground loop' occurs. (I would define a ground loop as an un-commanded, directional divergence.) If it does yaw off and you are quick enough to catch it, all you do is to stop the yaw then continue on that heading. Any attempt to correct back to the runway heading may lead to a ground loop in the other direction! The 109 is nasty on take-off; the Spitfire is much easier, but limited propeller tip clearance is a problem.

In flight

Both aircraft have very benign stall characteristics. The Spitfire is delightfully light to fly in pitch, although at aft c.g. positions it does become unstable but is still flyable. However, it is heavy in roll and has relatively light rudder forces. Therefore the controls are, in a classical sense, poorly harmonised. But despite this, it is still a joy to fly. It is worthy of note that of all of the Second World War fighters the Spitfire probably had the best controllability from very low speeds to very high speeds, and was controllable to a higher Mach number than any fighter of its era. The Bf109 is very heavy in pitch to the extent that it is inadvisable to trim out the elevator in high speed dives as the forces to pull out of the dive may be too great. It is lighter in roll than the Spitfire but with similar roll performance. Most versions of the 109 have no rudder trim so the pilot has to hold a rudder force, albeit light, most of the time. With respect to performance, it has always appeared to me that the 109 runs away from the Spitfire in a dive but that the Spitfire has the edge in turn performance, although the high stick forces in the 109 may be an influence on my perception of turn performance.

Approach and landing

In the circuit, the Spitfire is very straightforward with a single down selection of the pneumatically operated flaps, although the hydraulic undercarriage selector is awkward to operate. The forward view over the nose is poor, necessitating a curved approach to keep the runway in sight. The threshold speed is low (129kmh, 80mph, for a Mark V) and a 3-point landing is needed as the wing is still producing lift to a very low speed and a wheeled landing may result in the aircraft getting airborne again. Control power is excellent down to very low speeds, and I think that it is quite easy to land for this class of aircraft. The major problem is the potential for tipping it on its nose if you brake too hard. As for the 109, its flying qualities around the landing pattern are quite good, although the flaps take a lot of winding down by hand, and management of the propeller setting is more complex than the Spitfire. And then there is the landing! If I say that my finals checks are 'Gear down, flaps down, prop set, and please God may it roll straight on landing' you might get the picture. Put slightly more technically, it is very directionally unstable on the ground with a rudder that is ineffective with the power at idle and only weak directional control using differential braking due to the narrow track undercarriage. The locked tail wheel is the only item that gives some positive directional stability, and thus a three-point landing is essential. Also, these directional control characteristics lead to a much lower prudent crosswind limit in the 109 than in the Spitfire, and make operations from higher friction asphalt or concrete surfaces much less desirable.

Power for the Bf109

Two distinct types of engine were installed in the German-built Bf109s from the start of series production in 1936/37 until the end of German manufacture in 1945. These were the Junkers Jumo 210 series in the Bf109B, C and D series, and the Daimler-Benz DB600 series from the Bf109E onwards in the DB601 and later the DB605 series. Both manufacturers' engines were liquid-cooled, inverted 'V' 12-cylinder inline piston engines. All of the Daimler-Benz engines were fuel-injected (except for the carburettor-fed DB600), while the Jumo 210G was fuel-injected but the Jumo 210D had a normal carburettor fuel-feed system.

All engines fitted in the Bf109 of whatever mark were mounted on two engine bearer structures (one on each side of the engine), with these bearers fitted to the Bf109 fuselage at the firewall with four attachment points. Of these, the lower two attachment points also formed a part of the unique attachment of the main undercarriage legs to the fuselage structure. In the Jumo-engined Bf109s the engine bearers were of a welded steel tube structure, and in the Daimler-Benz powered Bf109s the more substantial engine bearers were manufactured from Elektron (cast magnesium alloy) with attendant tubular struts.

The fuel used for these engines depended on the specific mark of power plant, but was of either the B4 type of roughly 87 octane, or the nominally 100-octane C3 (actually the C3 was often of a lower octane rating of around 96). Later in the war, power boost systems were adopted for use in Luftwaffe fighters, and the versions of the Bf109 fitted with these systems used one of two types – GM 1 nitrous oxide, or MW 50 methanol-water. These power boost arrangements allowed extra output from the engine and therefore increased performance without having to resort to the trouble and time-consuming redesign of installing a new engine type into the Bf109 which in any case would have been impossible later in the war.

The original prototype of the Bf109 was powered by the Rolls-Royce Kestrel engine, but this was not intended for the production aircraft and was simply a stop-gap solution to get the prototype into the air. It was hoped by Messerschmitt that the Bf109 series would be powered by Daimler-Benz engines, but the more readily-available Jumo 210 instead powered the initial production versions of the Bf109 – the carburettor-equipped Jumo 210D of 680hp (this and all other hp ratings in this section refer to take-off power) in the Bf109B and Bf109D, and the fuel-injection Jumo 210G of 700hp in the Bf109C. These were comparatively simple engines of relatively low power output, and used B4 fuel (87 Octane).

From the Bf109E onwards the engine type switched to Daimler-Benz power. There were several prototype and development (or, in German, Versuchs) aircraft that were powered by the Daimler-Benz DB600 and have since mistakenly been identified as Bf109D production aircraft, but in reality no Bf109Ds were powered by the Daimler-Benz engines, and it was the Bf109E that introduced this type of power plant on the production line. The Daimler-Benz engines were supercharged, being able to derive additional power on demand from the supercharging system built into them which was air-driven and resulted in the installation of the prominent air intake on the left-hand side of the engine cowlings of the Bf109E and later versions. The DB601 had a relatively simple single-speed supercharger arrangement, while the DB605 series was fitted with a more effective single-stage variable-speed supercharger, although there were variations due to the fact that power boost was also available to some versions of the DB605 series engines.

The DB601A of 1,100hp powered most of the production Bf109E aircraft, and had been introduced into series manufacture as early as 1936. Developed from it and built from 1940 onwards, the DB601N was rated at 1,175hp and was installed in some later Bf109E versions and the Bf109F-1 and F-2 series. It had to use C3 100 octane fuel, whereas the DB601A would run quite happily on B4 fuel. The DB601E of 1,350hp was manufactured from 1939 and was installed in the Bf109F-3 and F-4 versions.

The DB601E was further developed from 1941 onwards into a new 600-series engine, the DB605, which powered many of the later production Bf109s. The initial production DB605A featured cylinder blocks of refined design and increased displacement, and other improvements such as an increase in the maximum allowable rpm to 2,800 (as opposed to some 2,600 in the earlier engines), and could produce 1,475hp when run with B4 fuel. It could also burn C3 100 octane fuel in conjunction with MW 50 boost to give 1,770hp. The latter configuration was known as the DB605AM engine. The DB605A powered all early versions of the Bf109G series, and therefore Black 6 was fitted with this type of engine. It was the same size dimensionally as the DB601, but was heavier by almost 60kg (132lb).

Further development led to the DB605AS, in production from 1944, which featured a refined supercharger of larger capacity and

ABOVE: **Two types of power-boost were employed for later versions of the Bf109. The GM1 nitrous oxide system was the most dangerous to ground crews, needing careful attention and protection for personnel during filling. Here a ground crew member fills the nitrous oxide concoction into a Bf109G. The starting handle for the engine can be seen protruding from the engine cowling ahead of the blister over the MG131 13mm machine gun installation.** *Peter Walter*

capability which gave greater performance for higher-altitude operations, for example on home defence duties against US bomber formations over Germany. Some examples of the Bf109G-5, G-6 and G-14 series were fitted with these engines, and were noted as such in their designations (e.g. Bf109G-6/AS). A version with MW 50 power boost also existed, as the DB605ASM.

The final wartime version of the DB605 to power Bf109s was the DB605D series, which retained the enlarged supercharger of the AS engines but also had a modified oil system with a higher compression ratio compared to the engines that went before it. A version that could be used in conjunction with MW 50 power boost also existed as the DB605DM. With a very creditable 2,000hp, the DB605D powered the final production versions of the Bf109, the Bf109G-10 and Bf109K-4, both of which used the MW 50 system. C3 100 Octane fuel had to be used with the MW 50 boosted engines, making these plus the Bf109 versions that were

fitted with the DB601N power plant the only Bf109 versions that specifically had to use that type of fuel, all other versions being able to fly with B4 (87 Octane) fuel.

The GM 1 power boost system aimed to give more power output from the engine for higher-level operations, and involved injecting nitrous oxide liquefied gas into the engine's supercharger. In its gaseous form this substance is sometimes known as 'laughing gas'. It was used as early as the Bf109E-7/Z version, and was housed in four containers located aft of the cockpit. In the Bf109F-4/Z and the pressurised Bf109G-1, the GM 1 was held in eight bottles, four in each wing. In the pressurised Bf109G-5 the GM 1 was stored in a large unarmoured 115-litre metal tank aft of the cockpit, with several compressed air bottles in the right-hand wing to feed the GM 1 into the supercharger. The latter installation was known as the U2 configuration, and was also retrofitted to some pressurised Bf109G-3 and unpressurised G-6 and G-8 versions as well.

For the somewhat different MW 50 methanol-water power boost system, on the other hand, a standardised installation was used in which an unarmoured 118-litre tank was fitted aft of the cockpit (some 85 litres of which was usable), which was filled through a filler cap located in the upper right-hand fuselage side above the tank. This system was more successful than the GM 1 installation, and the methanol-water was far less dangerous than the nitrous oxide of the GM 1 system. With the MW 50 injected directly into the supercharger a short-term increase of engine output of some 300hp could be achieved, but C3 100 octane fuel had to be used. The methanol-water could be made up in several mixes, the MW 50 using 50 per cent methanol and a similar MW 30 concoction using 30 per cent methanol (most of the rest was water). A related mixture used ethanol instead of methanol. The system was so successful that it was installed in many of the late-war Bf109 versions, starting with some Bf109G-6 but standardised in the G-10 and K-4.

Except for the Bf109B, some of which used a wooden propeller made by Schwarz, all Bf109s were fitted with metal VDM propellers. These were variable-pitch propellers, with

electric pitch change, and were always three-bladed units on production Bf109 versions from the Bf109E onwards. To take up the greater power output of the later DB605 engines, wide chord 'paddle' blades were developed. All Bf109G versions from the Bf109G-1 up to some G-14 used the VDM 9-12087 A version.

The foreign-built post-Second World War Bf109s had a variety of power plants, none of which the Bf109 had been designed for. Spanish Hispano Buchóns used two distinct and different power plants, initially by Hispano-Suiza and later from Rolls-Royce. Early production aircraft, of the HA-1112-K1L type, were powered by the Hispano-Suiza HS 12 Z 87/89 inline engine of 1,280hp. The later and more numerous HA-1112-M1L series were fitted with the Rolls-Royce Merlin 500-series engine. This power plant had a single-stage, two-speed supercharger and had been designed for civil airliner installation and operation, and could deliver 1,610hp.

In Czechoslovakia, although initial production

S-99 single-seater and CS-99 two-seater Bf109 lookalikes were powered by Daimler-Benz DB605 engines, as intended for the Bf109G series, later locally-produced and unlicensed Avia S-199 single-seater and two-seater CS-199 aircraft, were fitted with the completely unsuitable Junkers Jumo 211 engine. This liquid-cooled, inverted 'V' 12-cylinder inline piston engine had been designed primarily for bomber use, was bulky and turned in opposite rotation to the Daimler-Benz engines intended for the Bf109G series on which the S-199 and CS-199 were based. Known to the Czechs as the M-211, most of the Avia-built Jumo-engined aircraft used the M-211F of some 1,200hp. These aircraft were probably the worst production Bf109s of any type that were ever built, yet they nevertheless achieved a successful war record when exported examples flew for the Israelis in the later 1940s. Some of the Israeli-operated aircraft are believed to have been fitted with the slightly more powerful M-211J engine.

ABOVE: The post-war Czechoslovak-produced Avia S-199 and CS-199 were powered by an engine never before tried in the Bf109 airframe, the Junkers Jumo 211 (Czech M-211). This bulky, slow-responding bomber engine did nothing for the appearance, aerodynamics or performance of the resulting aircraft, which was certainly not a pilots' aeroplane. Here a Czech-operated S-199 shows that the Czechs retained the good engine access capability of the Bf109 line. *Jaroslav Matoulek Collection via 4+ Publishing Co*

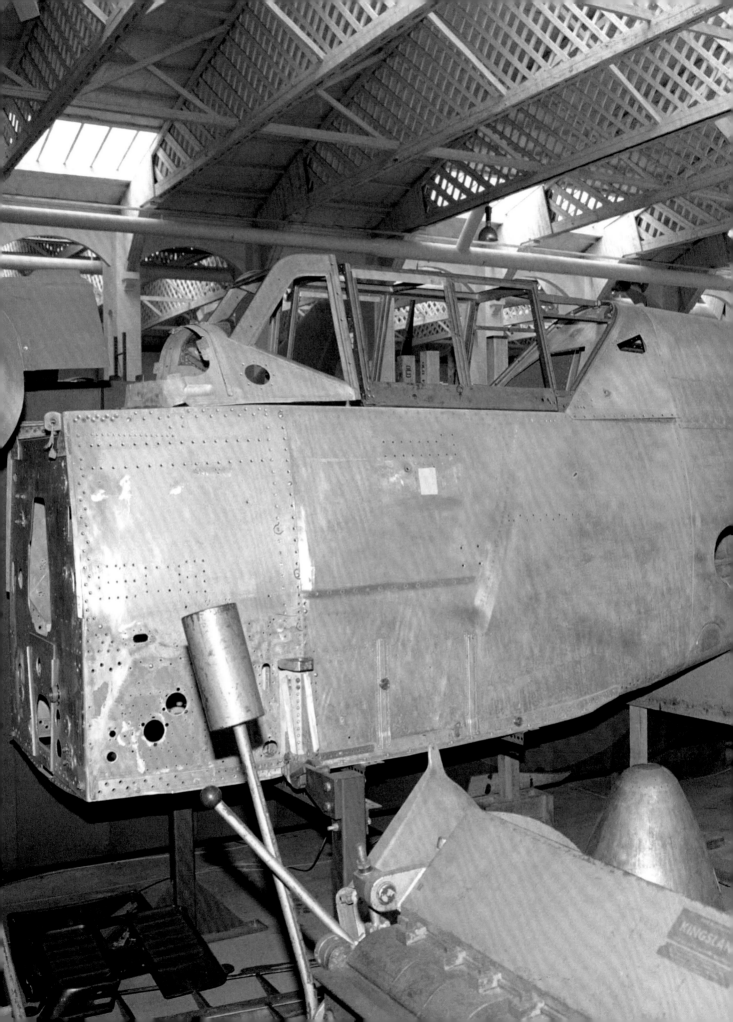

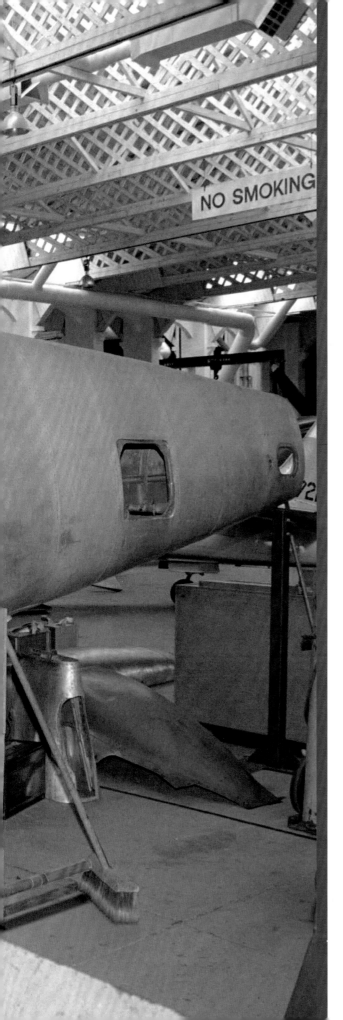

Chapter Two

Restore to flight

Owning any historic aircraft and maintaining it in airworthy condition is an expensive and time-consuming labour of love. Those who do this are dedicated enthusiasts and professionals, with deep pockets and seemingly limitless time and patience.

In addition, they need to have the back-up of a good team of engineers, and the goodwill of a wider base of individuals and companies who specialise in one or more of the dozens of skilled jobs that are required to put the many parts of an historic aircraft into perfect running order.

LEFT: Hispano HA-1112-M1L Buchón, (c/n 172), G-BWUE, at Duxford in April 1997 prior to restoration.

Added to this is the important issue of finding a display pilot to fly your historic aircraft – if you are not a suitably-rated pilot yourself – and the many (and often time-consuming and frustrating) issues of gaining the relevant and cherished airworthiness permits from your local civil aviation administrators.

Aircraft condition before restoration

Any historic aircraft that is sourced nowadays will be in very poor condition. Even one that has been kept inside will need extensive work and these finds are now very rare. The majority of new projects that emerge, most frequently from Eastern Europe, are wrecks that have been found in woodland or remote areas.

Sixty years of exposure to the elements and the fact that the aircraft, internally, had no surface finish on them (this was particularly true of later-war Bf109s, where the disintegrating production process in Nazi Germany was under increasing strain from Allied bombing), means that the aircraft would be heavily corroded. Items such as the tailplane and fin tips would probably have disappeared as they are magnesium and would have corroded more easily than the rest of the aircraft.

The propeller would have been damaged on impact, if the aircraft had crashed, and even if intact, would need extensive restoration as the hub and bearings would have corroded and seized.

The engine would, if exposed to the elements, be corroded and the ancillary drive at the back of the engine, being made of light alloy, could have corroded away completely. The engine would be seized and, due to corrosion between the steel and alloy parts, possibly be beyond restoration.

Valuable items, such as control column stick top, instruments, weapons etc., could well have been removed by souvenir hunters, possibly at the time of the crash.

Any rubber hoses, the fuel tank and any component internal seals could have perished and would probably fail any pressure test even if they appeared to be in reasonable condition.

Perspex on the canopy would either be cracked and beyond repair or, if intact, be of a milky appearance due to exposure to sunlight over a long period of time.

Repair, recondition or replace?

If you buy a wreck that has been in a field or barn for over 60 years you are, without a doubt, going to have to replace more of your aircraft than you can actually restore. Sourcing original Bf109 parts would be extremely difficult, if not impossible. However, using the original pieces as a pattern, it is possible to have new parts made.

Where instrumentation is concerned, it is up to individual choice whether modern instruments are used within the cockpit, or whether originals are sourced, at great expense, or perhaps a combination of both may be chosen.

Items such as rubber seals for valves and jacks are still available commercially, as are many Messerschmitt hydraulic components and fasteners, as these items are all used on Pilatus aircraft.

Propeller blades are still made by Hoffmann, in Germany, although they are now manufactured of laminated wood instead of metal. Ironically, the company also produces Spitfire propeller blades.

Tyres and tubes are available from Dunlop and although not original, they are roughly the same size and fit the wheels safely.

How do refurbished Bf109s differ from their original state?

This question is as relevant for the Bf109 as it is for all other airworthy historic aircraft. As can be seen from the history of Black 6 elsewhere in this book, many of the aircraft's original parts were lost over the course of time. This process started during the war when the aircraft had to be returned to airworthy condition having been discovered abandoned in late 1942 at Gambut Main airfield. Original parts continued to disappear after the aircraft came to England

and was repaired following damage sustained before it reached its new owners at RAF Collyweston. Subsequently, during its year or so of active flying in Britain, the aircraft had a number of problems which needed rectifying – again leading to original components having to be replaced. The hard years for this aircraft, however, were following the end of the Second World War, when souvenir hunters stole important parts, and at least one half-hearted attempt at restoration resulted in more harm than good being done to the Messerschmitt. On the other hand, the excellent standard of work that was performed on Black 6 after Russ Snadden began to rescue it from the early 1970s ensured that some of the original parts were restored to the aircraft, although others had to come from elsewhere. Then, following the Messerschmitt's untimely accident in 1997, a major rebuild was necessary in which a number of components had to be sourced from elsewhere too – including vertical tail and rear fuselage parts.

In general configuration, however, it must be stressed that Black 6 was – and is to this day – a genuine Bf109G, without a hint of Hispano Buchón to darken its name during its flying career. Airframe and engine were completely genuine German Second World War components, with as many genuine parts sourced by Russ Snadden's team as possible during the very lengthy restoration of the aircraft back to airworthy configuration. In detail, this was also true, apart from the aircraft having a radio where the rounds counter box should have been fitted and an E2B compass where the gunsight mounting beam would have been located. The original radio was never fitted back into the rear fuselage while Black 6 was flying, however it has since been relocated. The ammunition boxes and feed chutes were also not installed – and of course no working guns were fitted, in line with the requirements of all ex-military aircraft that are in private hands for air show appearances and public display.

In Germany, the restored and sometimes airworthy Bf109/Buchón composites can be seen as a half-way house towards a genuine Bf109 configuration. These aircraft, operated by the EADS and Messerschmitt Stiftung (Foundation) at Manching, are – like many existing 'Bf109s' – actually part genuine Bf109 and part Hispano Buchón. The same is true for several non-flying museum exhibits around the world, although there are notable exceptions: the ex-JG 26 Bf109E, Werk Nummer 1190, that is on display

ABOVE: This ex-JG26 Bf109E, Werk Nummer 1190, is on display at the Imperial War Museum, Duxford, and is a genuine Battle of Britain veteran. Absolutely genuine Bf109s like this aircraft are rare, but the end of the Cold War has seen a number of wrecks being recovered from crash sites in Russia for possible restoration. *Malcolm V. Lowe*

at the Imperial War Museum at Duxford is a genuine Battle of Britain veteran that has also had a hard life following its capture, but is now displayed in a diorama setting representing its untimely arrival on its belly after combat.

Airframe

Once retrieved, there are very few people who you can go to to have your airframe restored to flying condition. Companies such as Charleston Aviation Services in conjunction with Airframe Assemblies, and EADS in Germany (successor to the Messerschmitt and MBB companies), would be a good place to start.

Engine

Sourcing an original Daimler-Benz DB605 engine is, in keeping with the possibility of finding a genuine Bf109 airframe in good condition, nowadays very unlikely. There are many examples of displayed Daimler-Benz engines in museums that could form the basis of a complete rebuild, although the necessary rigours of modern inspection and airworthiness requirements mean that such work is rightly a long and expensive process. Work on bringing back to life the DB605A engine of Black 6 was a lengthy and difficult process which involved a great deal of help from outside organisations. Rolls-Royce employees at Filton proved to be an excellent source of help for the Black 6 project.

It is, however, a different situation with regard to the Hispano Buchón. In this case there is the much easier possibility of sourcing Rolls-Royce Merlin engines. Although they are becoming increasingly rare, the easiest route by far to owning a 109 is to go down this path. There is also a good knowledge base and engineering facilities where the Merlin engine is concerned – there are currently many Merlins of several different marks flying in airworthy Spitfires, Hurricanes and Mustangs, and so the back-up for engineering, know-how and spares exists to a much greater degree than for the DB605.

Electrical system

Complete rewiring would be necessary. Provided you have all the appropriate plugs, sockets and circuit breakers, the wiring system is straightforward as long as you have the relevant manual with associated diagrams.

Hydraulic system

All the hoses would have to be replaced and the metal pipework would need pressure testing to see if it was fit for use. Valves and jack assemblies would need stripping down and checking for internal corrosion with all seals being replaced and pressure tested.

Cockpit instrumentation

As previously mentioned, original instruments can be obtained, but the price is high. The instrument panel can be remade in order to accommodate modern instrumentation, however this will also mean changing plugs and sockets.

Original instruments will contain radioactive luminous paint and care should be taken if any instrument has the glass front broken and advice sought when disposing of instruments regardless of condition.

Undercarriage

The undercarriage should be stripped down, seals replaced and if intact but not good enough to use, there are companies which will manufacture new seals to pattern. The bore of the casing should be checked for corrosion, as it may be possible to hone out any light corrosion. The casing and axles should be checked for cracks using NDT. Condition of the fescalised plunger tube should be noted, if pitted and corroded they can be ground back and replated as long as the corrosion is not too deep. It is possible to get newer undercarriage legs that, with minor alterations, will fit. These are available from the Pilatus P2 aircraft.

Radio/navigation fit

A modern radio, VHF, will have to be fitted in accordance with today's requirements. The original compass and repeater, if in working order, will suffice, however a modern replacement would be acceptable. An IFF system is now required to be fitted in accordance with modern regulations.

AID inspection

Once your project is completed you will have to show the CAA that all materials have come from approved sources and that the companies that worked on your aircraft are approved.

All paperwork regarding materials and work should be retained for future reference and you

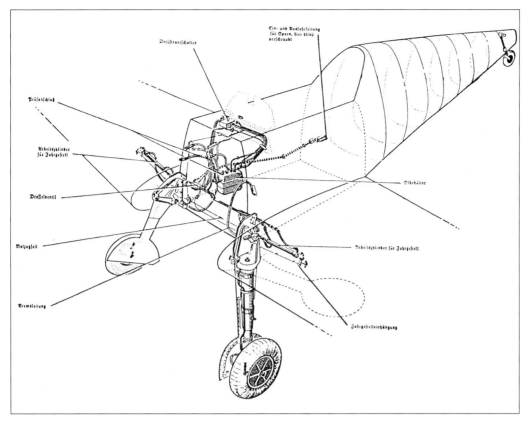

LEFT: The main undercarriage of the Bf109 was designed to fit onto the fuselage and was not attached in the wings, thereby allowing the wings to be removed for ease of movement by rail. The fuselage was intended to stand on its main undercarriage with the wings removed, and could easily be towed in a dismantled state. This illustration from a contemporary Bf109 manual shows the main undercarriage attachment and operating system. *Messerschmitt AG/ Malcolm V. Lowe*

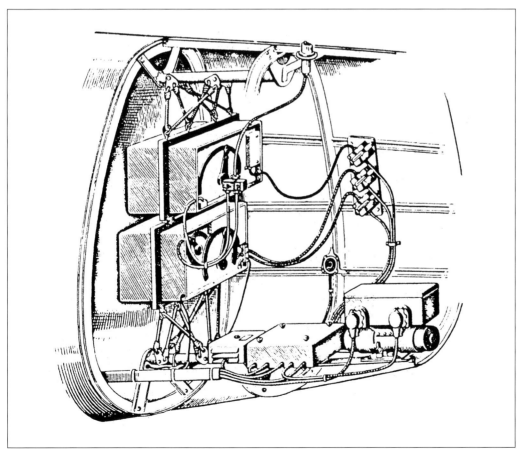

LEFT: The main radio equipment in the Bf109 series was normally located in the rear fuselage. This drawing is from a Bf109E manual. It shows the general arrangement that was similar from the Bf109B through to the early Bf109G series, and would therefore have been applicable to Bf109G-2 Black 6. Each main box of the FuG VII/VIIa equipment was supported by rubber cords which absorbed some of the vibration and knocks that this sensitive equipment would receive in the course of normal flying, and at take-off and on landing. *Messerschmitt AG/Malcolm V. Lowe*

RIGHT: The Buchón cockpit of G-BWUE pictured here is complete with modern avionics equipment and some modern instruments.

should be able to show that you have a laid down procedure for operating and servicing your aircraft. The aircraft should have a log book for logging flying hours and a log book for recording engine hours.

After passing these stringent guidelines, you should receive a permit to test, which enables you to flight test your aircraft and once this is complete you should then be able to obtain your permit to fly. This allows the aircraft to display.

Modern safety requirements

Aircraft are now required to carry a VHF radio and an IFF system. An in-date, serviceable parachute is also a necessity. Items such as flexible hoses (fuel and oil) are now 'lifed' and require pressure testing every six years.

Rebuilding the Emil:
Steve Vizard

Steve Vizard is the owner of Airframe Assemblies, on the Isle of Wight. The company restores Spitfire and Bf109 airframes for customers worldwide. He is interested in aviation archaeology, and has taken part in numerous digs, including the excavation of a crashed 1940-vintage Spitfire in northern France that was televised on the Channel 4 documentary series Time Team. *Here he recalls the trials and successes of restoring a Bf109E for Craig Charleston, who is himself a leading light in the small but dedicated field of breathing life into derelict Bf109 airframes.*

The necessity to restore the airframe for a Bf109E came about in the early 1990s when Craig Charleston acquired the first intact E model to emerge from Russia. Although substantially complete, the airframe did need to be totally stripped and restored, and new parts had to be made where original structure was either missing or damaged beyond repair and so necessitated replacement to ensure safety and integrity.

The remit for the restoration was therefore to recreate the ability to produce the replacement parts as required by duplicating the original manufacturing procedures and methods.

The German aircraft industry in the 1930s adopted a quite different outlook from the British. Whereas most British aircraft companies seemingly had an abundance of labour, the methods of production involved less tooling and more people – the Germans were far quicker to adopt substantial tooling as the way forward to mass production, with less labour being required for that process. For example, a typical Spitfire wing rib can comprise of 20, 30, 40 or more detail parts, whereas a similar rib on the Bf109 wing is a one-piece pressing.

The fuselage construction is also more straightforward than a Spitfire or Hurricane equivalent, due again to the stretch formed frame shells and roll formed stringer section being the only basic components necessary.

This was achievable *only* due to the level of press and form tools adopted as the method of manufacture, and again differed markedly from the myriad of detail parts used in the construction of most British types.

Upon being given the contract to restore the airframe for Craig's first 109, we then had to work out how to do it. The structure that was obviously salvageable did not present a problem, but the replacement and repair parts that we were going to need did provide a challenge.

We were lucky in the respect that Airframe Assemblies had access to a large quantity of Battle of Britain wreckology parts gathered in the 1970s, and utilising this source of information as pattern examples gave many details on profiles/ dimensions/gauges and so forth, and all these items were then redrawn to allow that information to be used – necessary to comply with the extant CAA requirements both then and now.

This store of original parts did not tell us much about the airframe as an entity, however, and we needed much more technical knowledge if we were to restore the fuselage and wings. Through the services of several established contacts in Europe – thank you Jean M. – we gathered copies of the crucial documentation from which, along with sources in the UK, we could establish material types, heat treatment procedures and everything necessary that had to be put in place in order to (a) have the ability to undertake the work, and (b) to satisfy the CAA conditions under which we operate.

We were fortunate to then gain, after much time, effort and expenditure, a set of E model

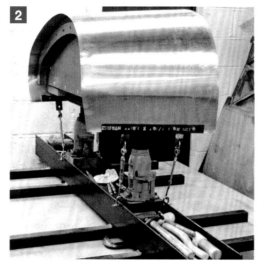

1 Skin former.
2 Skin on former.
3 Skin being formed.
4 Formed skin section.
5 Completed skin panels.

Airframe Assemblies

drawings which had to be the precursor of making the huge stretch form tools that the fuselage shells are made on. Craig then sanctioned the manufacture of the form tools, itself a very time-consuming and expensive process, and some trial runs were completed. Due to the complexity of the frame flanges and return joggled edges, the skins have to be pulled and formed in a softened condition, then heat treated when finished. The only sure way to negate potential distortion when the frames are quenched after treatment is the use of a 360° spray system, and we were fortunate in having subcontract access to such specialised equipment right on our doorstep – without this, the task would be much, much harder.

The rear fuselage section was then rebuilt, adopting the methods as described, and the information and technical/material knowledge that we continued to accrue enabled all the rest of the fuselage, main planes and airframe components to be restored, repaired or replaced, as required.

The sheet metal skills that are needed to make these replacement parts cannot be underestimated, and these 'old' skills must not be allowed to fade as all modern aircraft structures become increasingly more composite. The assembly too of these parts into wings and fuselages is a demanding task,

ABOVE: Fuselage half, internal view. *Airframe Assemblies*

RIGHT: Fuselage half, external view. *Airframe Assemblies*

and we are fortunate at Airframe Assemblies to have a highly skilled and knowledgeable workforce, which is absolutely necessary to achieve this level of restoration.

It should be borne in mind that, until Craig embarked on this rebuild, no one had seriously attempted to build a genuine 109E in any airworthy context whatever, and as for the production of items such as fuselage panels – this was unheard of and was therefore the first time these parts had been made since the original production stopped.

Over the next few years, the aircraft was restored to fly, and took to the air for the first time in California in 1998.

We have since rebuilt five other 109 fuselages – and wings – including, of course, the rear cone repair for Black 6, as well as supplying parts at Craig's discretion to other projects around the world.

The cost of restoring/rebuilding the airframe of a 109, as with most other rare and desirable types, is considerable, but the end value will always exceed the build cost by a considerable margin, so these aircraft are a sound investment for those fortunate few lucky enough to own a piece of history.

The initial set-up expenses required in order to 'reinvent the wheel' and tool up for rebuilding 109s was high, and Craig took the decision

early on that no compromises were permissible, everything *had* to be exactly as it was originally, and he should be commended for that resolve, for while we have made just about every jig, block and tool needed for Spitfire parts over a 25-year span and our inventory has increased gradually, the 109 operation required the majority of tooling to be available in no more than a couple of years, which in itself was a major achievement.

A comprehensive knowledge of wartime German materials has also been built up over the years, and again this has been no small task as existing archive documentation had to be translated (when we could find it, and in many cases there was no reference) then a pattern original part was tested to give mechanical breakdown and chemical properties so an equivalent and acceptable substitute could be found – once again, a process that has to adhere to the approval conditions set by the CAA.

Over 15 years later it is not uncommon to see photographs of the 109E flying, and now perhaps it does not provoke the reaction that it once did, and might again when we finally see one in the skies over the UK, but the sense of satisfaction and achievement of having had a major involvement with Craig in getting these aircraft back in the air is something that I, and the skilled workforce at Airframe Assemblies, are still very proud of.

LEFT: Bf109E wing under construction.
Airframe Assemblies

Chapter Three

The Black 6 Story

The famous Messerschmitt Bf109G-2/Trop Black 6 became a much-loved and easily recognisable aircraft on the air display circuit during the 1990s.

Unique at that time in being the only genuine Messerschmitt fighter of the Second World War era in airworthy condition, the aircraft was only airworthy at all because of the dedication and sheer hard work of a small group of enthusiasts whose tireless devotion to the cause – in the face of what sometimes amounted to official indifference – resulted in the unforgettable sight of a real Bf109G in the air.

LEFT: Displaying all the grace and beauty of a fine combat aircraft, Black 6 makes an impressive sight. The photograph was taken during the Messerschmitt's heyday, following years of painstaking restoration that brought life back to this rare and historic aircraft. *Richard Paver*

History of Black 6

The famed Messerschmitt Bf109G-2 Black 6 is without doubt one of the most recognisable and best-known of the restored Second World War aircraft that have graced the skies of Britain in recent years. This iconic aircraft is a true survivor, having lived through combat in the Second World War and persisted in the decades afterwards when many historic aircraft were sadly and thoughtlessly scrapped. The fact that Black 6 is no longer airworthy is in no way a fault of the dedicated and skilled craftsmen who worked so hard to restore this historic aircraft to flying status and maintain it in airworthy condition until its untimely grounding through an unfortunate accident and lack of funding from official sources.

Black 6 was built by Erla Maschinenwerk GmbH of Leipzig in September 1942. Erla was one of the various sub-contractors which were involved in Bf109 manufacture during the Second World War, under the direction of the Messerschmitt parent company. The aircraft was allocated the Werk Nummer (manufacturer's/constructor's airframe serial or construction number) of 10639, and the Stammkennzeichen (four-letter 'factory code' for radio call and identification purposes) PG+QJ. This code was painted on Luftwaffe aircraft for factory testing, acceptance and delivery flights, but would have been painted out en route to or on arrival at the operational unit allocated to the aircraft and the identification replaced by the relevant unit-level recognition – which as we know in the case of Werk Nummer 10639 was to be Black 6.

After successful factory test flying (unfortunately the name of the Erla test pilot who first flew the aircraft has never been identified), 10639 was formally accepted by the Luftwaffe on 13 October 1942. On 21 October it was picked up by a pilot of the IIIrd Gruppe of Luftwaffe fighter wing JG 77 (III./JG 77), which gave a clue as to its intended theatre of operations – elements of JG 77 were at that time stationed in North Africa. Indeed, 10639 is actually a Bf109G-2/Trop, meaning that it was 'tropicalised' for operations in sandy or dusty environments, the most obvious representation of this modification being the prominent filter attached to the supercharger air intake on the left-hand side of the engine cowling. The aircraft then embarked on a long delivery flight, with München-Riem in southern Germany, Vicenza and then Jesi, Foggia, and Bari in Italy being its next ports of call. It is believed that the Messerschmitt's Stammkennzeichen were painted out during its stop-over at Bari, and its famous Black 6 painted on the fuselage sides. The delivery flight continued until 3 November when the aircraft arrived at Quasaba in Cyrenaica. Its arrival coincided with a black period for the Axis forces in North Africa. British and Commonwealth forces had successfully blunted the Axis drive towards Alexandria in Egypt, and the battle of El Alamein had commenced a long retreat for the German and Italian forces.

Black 6 was at once caught up in this retreat, and staged back to Bir el Aba landing ground where some of JG 77's resources were temporarily stationed. On 4 November Black 6 at last flew a combat sortie, although its pilot was apparently injured during this action. It is known that a pilot of III./JG 77 who flew Black 6 was Leutnant Heinz Ludemann, and that the aircraft was on the books of the 8th Staffel of JG 77 (8./JG 77), which was one of the Staffeln within the 3rd Gruppe of JG 77. It appears that the damage sustained by Black 6 on this or other flights at around this time necessitated the

BELOW: One of JG77's Bf109G-2s forms the backdrop for this group photo of Luftwaffe airmen from III./JG77. Although the aircraft in the picture is not Black 6, this view gives a good indication of what Black 6 would have looked like during its brief combat career. Standing fourth from the left just below the aircraft's spinner is Heinz Ludemann who flew Black 6 in combat. *Black 6 Team*

aircraft being flown to Gambut Main (a major Landing Ground, LG 139), where the Germans had repair facilities for repair work that could not be carried out immediately in the field. Time had run out for the Germans in that part of Cyrenaica, however, and on 12/13 November the area around the airfield was taken over by Commonwealth forces. Black 6 was among the trawl of German aircraft that were discovered there.

Some of the personnel of No. 3 Squadron, Royal Australian Air Force, took up residence at Gambut Main and an engineering officer of that unit, Flight Lieutenant Ken McRae, looked over Black 6. He and Squadron Leader R.H. Gibbes realised that the aircraft was practically brand new, and would most probably be of use to Allied intelligence. The early versions of the Bf109G were at that time of great interest to the Allies. The Bf109G was a comparatively new mark of Bf109 which clearly had greater capability than previous versions, and posed a new threat particularly at that time in North Africa where it was being increasingly encountered by Allied warplanes. Black 6 was one of the first Gustavs to be captured in good condition by Allied forces, and as such the aircraft was of considerable interest and great technical value. Unfortunately some important items, such as the armament and it is believed the gunsight, had apparently been removed by the Germans before the airfield was abandoned – although the removal of the centrally-mounted MG 151/20 cannon would have been a major exercise. Members of the engineering staff of No. 3 Squadron subsequently made Black 6 flyable by removing the necessary items from other, less airworthy Gustavs at Gambut Main, and the aircraft had its German identity markings overpainted. In their place were RAF roundels and the fuselage coding CV-V with 'CV' being the squadron code letters for No. 3 Squadron.

Black 6 was flown to Gazala (LG 150) in Egypt on 15 November 1942, still near to the front line and only days after its capture. Four days later it moved on to Martuba, and on 2 December it was flown to Cairo (Heliopolis). There appears to have been some thought that the aircraft might have been intended for transportation on to Australia as a 'war prize', but it was instead valued by Allied intelligence

ABOVE: Black 6 takes to the air under new ownership. Following its capture at Gambut Main in November 1942 by 3 Squadron, Royal Australian Air Force, the aircraft had its German markings and insignia over-painted and the code letters 'CV–V' applied. (The code letters 'CV' were assigned to 3 Squadron.) It is believed that piloting the aircraft on this occasion at Gambut was Squadron Leader R.H. Gibbes of 3 Squadron. *Black 6 Team*

and in mid-December 1942 it was flown to Lydda in Palestine. From late December 1942 it was flown by several evaluation and test pilots, and was looked after by personnel of No. 451 Squadron, Royal Australian Air Force. One of the pilots who was fortunate to fly Black 6 at that time was Ronald Harker of Rolls-Royce, who is credited for being the first person to correctly realise earlier that year that re-engining the Allison-engined North American Mustang with the Rolls-Royce Merlin would make a superlative all-round fighter aircraft. Another well-known pilot to take Black 6 up for evaluation was Wing Commander G. Mungo

BELOW: Black 6 following its capture. By the time this picture was taken, the aircraft had been partly repainted 'in the field' with the code letters 'CV–V' applied, but it still wears part of its German camouflage scheme with all the German markings over-painted. *Black 6 Team*

ABOVE: Black 6 makes an impressive sight in this late Second World War air-to-air photograph when the aircraft was with the RAF's 1426 Flight. *Black 6 Team*

BELOW: Black 6 was allocated the British military serial number RN228 in late 1943, and was completely repainted in British camouflage colours after its arrival in Britain. *Black 6 Team*

Buxton, whose test flights in the aircraft allowed much data to be obtained as to the type's performance and capabilities. Clearly Black 6 was a very important aircraft at that time.

The following few months are somewhat shrouded in mystery, but it is known that Black 6 was ferried back to Egypt where it appears to have come on to the books of No.107 MU at Kasfereet. After a period of apparent inactivity the aircraft was shipped to England through the port of Liverpool. It subsequently arrived in crates at RAF Collyweston in Northamptonshire on 26 December 1943. This airfield was the home of many captured Axis aircraft and was where the RAF's No.1426 Flight was located. This unit flew enemy aircraft for evaluation purposes and displayed them at operational bases to allow Allied airmen to get up close to

the enemy that they faced. Unfortunately the crates that Black 6 had been packed in were found to be damaged on arrival at Collyweston, and it was some time before the aircraft was made flyable. It is possible that parts from another former JG 77 Bf109G-2/Trop that arrived in the same consignment as Black 6, Werk Nummer 10533, might have been used to make the aircraft flyable. The work to make Black 6 airworthy took some time to complete, and the aircraft flew for the first time in Britain at Collyweston on 19 February 1944. It was allocated during November 1943 the British military serial number RN228, which was painted on the airframe to go with the RAF-style camouflage and British national insignia that adorned the aircraft during the latter stages of the war. From 24 February until 7 March the Messerschmitt was flown in performance trials against examples of various Allied aircraft types, including a Hawker Tempest Mk.V, Supermarine Seafire, and North American Mustang Mk.III. Interestingly, a prominent conclusion from the trials in comparison with the Mustang was that most of the other types involved had 'no endurance' – the Mustang had the greatest endurance on internal fuel of any Allied or Axis fighter in the Second World War.

Subsequently Black 6 became a regular visitor to air bases up and down England while flying with No.1426 Flight. It was flown by RAF pilots. Some of these trips were eventful, and a number of problems were encountered. During March 1944 the aircraft had a take-off accident and dropped its right-hand wing-tip into the ground in an incident reminiscent of many other similar Bf109 accidents. Fortunately a full ground-loop did not occur, but a new wing-tip had to be found. On another occasion a propeller blade was damaged, necessitating all three blades being slightly shortened to maintain balance, something that would never be allowed in these more safety-conscious days. A serious engine problem was encountered in April 1944 necessitating a complete engine change. Nevertheless, Black 6 performed its role of familiarising Allied pilots with the Bf109G layout in the air and on the ground all over the country until the early part of 1945, when this role became increasingly

LEFT: **Black 6 was not very well looked after from the later 1950s onwards, and at one stage masqueraded as 'White 14' in spurious German camouflage and markings. A number of parts disappeared from the aircraft during that time including its original tail wheel. The highly inappropriate 'replacement' can be seen in this photograph that was taken during the 1960s at RAF Wattisham.**
Black 6 Team

irrelevant as the Allies swept towards victory in Europe. No.1426 Flight was disbanded in January 1945 and on 27 March 1945 Black 6 was transferred to the Enemy Aircraft Flight of the Central Fighter Establishment (CFE) at RAF Tangmere in Sussex.

The war in Europe ended quietly for Black 6, and with the coming of peace the aircraft became essentially redundant. Fortunately its status at the CFE resulted in it being absent from the scrapping that befell a large number of German aircraft that had been brought to Britain during and just after the war, and on 1 November 1945 the aircraft was officially transferred for storage at No. 47 MU at RAF Sealand. In fact, the Air Historical Branch had taken an interest in the Messerschmitt, and it was actually transferred to Sealand in the spring of 1946. During the coming decade Black 6 was used for public display purposes, appearing at several Battle of Britain Week displays in Horse Guards Parade in London from 1949 and being on the books of various other RAF airfields including No.15 MU at Wroughton, near Swindon in Wiltshire, and RAF Cranwell. Unfortunately during this period the aircraft was repainted in very crude 'German' markings. Black 6 started to deteriorate at this time, but fortunately there was apparently no serious thought of scrapping this increasingly rare and valuable aircraft.

In September 1961 Black 6 was transferred to RAF Wattisham, Suffolk, where attempts were made to start to restore the aircraft. These were, sadly, disastrous, and many original parts were lost, with some being replaced with non-standard items. There is an oft-repeated tale that the Messerschmitt was even fitted with a Spitfire tailwheel. It was during this period that the aircraft languished in highly dubious colours as 'Yellow 14', purporting to represent one of the Bf109s piloted by the legendary Luftwaffe ace pilot Hans-Joachim Marseille, who flew the type in combat in North Africa. In keeping with the non-standard appearance that it was increasingly gaining, Black 6 was fitted with a late-war Erla Haube (the so-called 'Galland Hood'), with which it was most definitely not equipped during its combat period in North Africa. By that time the aircraft had also gained a military ground maintenance serial number, 8478M.

Luckily, wiser heads eventually prevailed. In the early 1970s Flight Lieutenant Russ Snadden, who was to have such a profound influence on Black 6's subsequent history, became acquainted with the Messerschmitt. He had been intending to restore one of the (sadly by then) few in number surviving former Luftwaffe aircraft that still existed in Britain, and approaches to the right authorities resulted in Black 6 being airlifted in a Lockheed C-130 Hercules transport aircraft from Wattisham to RAF Lyneham in Wiltshire where he was then stationed. That took place on 30 September 1972, and Snadden's initiative brought together a small but dedicated team who subsequently worked on the aircraft to such a high standard.

ABOVE: Black 6 at RAF Benson following the lengthy restoration by Russ Snadden and his colleagues. By then she looked much more like her former self. *Black 6 Team*

BELOW: DB601E engine cutaway. *DB601 Spares Manual, 1941*

Among them was Paul Blackah, co-author on this book.

Black 6 had to follow Russ Snadden to his subsequent postings, including RAF Northolt in 1975 and during 1983 to RAF Benson in Oxfordshire. A great deal of help was made available during this long period by many individuals and several companies to aid the restoration of Black 6 and its Daimler-Benz DB605A engine. It was a very long process with numerous potential setbacks, and considerable detective work was required to try to track down items that had been removed from the aircraft on previous 'restoration' attempts. Finally, in mid-1990 the work was coming to a conclusion, and on 8 July 1990 Black 6's engine was run in the

airframe for the first time in many years. It was still some time before the first post-restoration flight could be made, but a British civil registration, G-USTV, was allocated in October 1990.

At Benson on 17 March 1991, Black 6 took to the air for the first time since 1945. The first flight was successfully accomplished by Group Captain Reg Hallam – although the Messerschmitt almost bit back by swinging on take-off in true Bf109 fashion. Some damage was sustained by the propeller during this incident and the second flight was not made until 12 July 1991. Black 6 was duly flown to its new home, the famous Duxford airfield in Cambridgeshire which was already by then the mecca for airworthy historic aircraft preservation in Britain. Although still technically a military aircraft on the books of the RAF, and actually delegated to the Imperial War Museum for civil registration and operational purposes, Black 6 received no official funding through its lengthy restoration, and indeed very little official help of any kind. To this end it was always probable that Black 6's air display life would be limited, and during the 1990s the fate of the aircraft remained in doubt. At first intended to be grounded in 1994, this was eventually extended to 1997, with the Imperial War Museum through its substantial Duxford presence still being responsible for the aircraft's operation – although Russ Snadden and his small but dedicated team continued to perform the day-to-day work on the aircraft.

Power for Black 6

The heart of the Bf109 was its engine. In the case of Black 6 this was the Daimler-Benz DB605A, which was one of the leading inline fighter engines of its day. Unlike the Rolls-Royce Merlin, the DB605-series engines were fuel-injected, allowing the Bf109s fitted with these power plants to fly and fight upside down if need be, something that early marks of the Spitfire found impossible during the Battle of Britain – the Merlin was designed to have a carburettor fuel system which prevented Spitfires and Hurricanes from flying inverted for any length of time due to fuel starvation in that attitude.

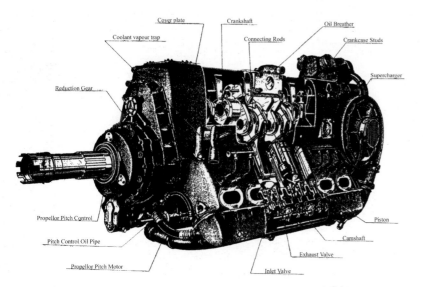

Daimler-Benz DB605A

Cylinder arrangement

Number of cylinders	12
Bore	154mm
Stroke	160mm
Displacement of cylinder	2.99 litres
Total displacement	approx. 35.7 litres
Compression volume	0.48 litres
Compression ratio	1:7.3 left-hand cylinder
	1:7.5 right-hand cylinder
Arrangement	2 cylinder blocks 60° angle inverted V

Valves

Number inlet valves per cylinder	2
Number of outlet valves per cylinder	2
Valve timing	The setting is based on a valve timing at the start of the opening of the double cam = 67° from bottom dead centre (+/- 1.0° clearance) for the 1st and 7th cylinders
Valve stroke	13.6 mm (without valve clearance)
Valve clearance	(for the cold engine) between valve and tappet
	Inlet 0.3mm
	Outlet 0.6mm

Magneto ignition

Design	Bosch twin magneto ignition
Type	ZM 12 CR 8, part #9-4040E
Type of ignition timing adj.	(a) Mechanical, as a function of the throttle lever position
	(b) Manually retarded ignition for cleaning spark plugs. Automatic switch-back to function (a) after releasing the operating lever
Direction of rotation	Right-hand
Firing order	1, 8, 5, 10, 3, 7, 6, 11, 2, 9, 4, 12,1

Spark plugs

Quantity	2 per cylinder
Manufacturer	Bosch DW250 ET 7
Screening	Yes

Inertia starter

Manufacturer	Bosch
Type	AL SED AR 1 for pure manual operation

Supercharger

Manufacturer	Daimler-Benz
Supercharger pressure	Take-off and emergency rating 1.42 atmospheres
Pressure in front of valves	Climb and combat rating 1.30 atmospheres. Max. permissible endurance rating 1.15 atmosphere

Boost pressure control

Manufacturer	Daimler-Benz
Mode of operation	Automatic throttling of the air supply to max. permissible pressure

Fuel feed pump

Manufacturer	Ehrich and Graetz
Type	Graetzin pump ZD 500
Quantity	1
Delivery capacity	Approx 970 l/h on the ground at 2,600rpm of the crankshaft (approx 485 l/h each side)
Fuel pressure	1.3-1.8kg/cm^2

Injection pump

Manufacturer	Bosch, Stuttgart
Quantity	1
Type	PZ 12 HP 110/25, part # 9-2196 C-1 with mixture control EP/HB 52/14 and float vent FP/LQ 300/3
Direction of rotation	Left-hand rotation, viewed on drive end
Speed	½ crankshaft rpm
Number of elements	12
Piston stroke	10mm
Piston diameter	11mm
Max. delivery capacity per element per stroke	650mm^3
Control rod travel	21mm
Arrangement of the elements	Inverted
Numbering of elements	12, 11, 10, 6, 5, 4, 3, 2, 1, 9, 8, 7
Injection sequence of elements (= engine firing order)	1, 8, 5, 10, 3, 7, 6, 11, 2, 9, 4, 12
Start of delivery	48°+/- 2° from top dead centre (suction stroke)
Oil capacity (in the mixture control housing)	1,200cm^3
Oil pressure	to leakage stop 4kg/cm^2
	to servo motor 8kg/cm^2

Injection nozzle

Type	L'Orange 9-2137G and 9-2261B
Quantity	1 per cylinder

Oil pressure pump on engine

Manufacturer	Daimler-Benz
Design	Gear pump
Rate of delivery	58 litres/min at 2,600 crankshaft rpm and 75° inlet temperature

Scavenge oil pump

Manufacturer	Daimler-Benz
Quantity	One per cylinder head
Design	Double gear pump
Delivery at 2600 crankshaft RPM	Pump on left-hand cylinder block = 47kg/min
	Pump on right-hand cylinder block = 41.5kg/min

Coolant pump on engine

Manufacturer	Daimler-Benz
Design	Centrifugal pump
Delivery	According to back pressure, 3,200 to 7,200 litres/hour at 2,600rpm

Tachogenerator

Quantity	1
Direction of rotation	Clockwise viewed on drive end of tachometer
Reduction gear ratio	2:1

What can go wrong?

The most common problems facing a Bf109 are related to take-off and landing. These were well documented throughout its service and are referred to elsewhere in this book. Several restorations have been harmed in this way, resulting in propeller, undercarriage and wing damage. The usual snags that can arise with every historic aircraft also affect the Bf109, including leaking pipe joints, worn seals, gauges and temperature bulbs failing.

As Black 6 was the first genuine Bf109 to fly since the Second World War, there were a few unusual teething problems; the starter clutch unit was not torqued to the correct setting, causing the engine to be difficult to start. This was followed by over adjusting and the engine would start; however, it placed a lot of loading on the fitting attached to the back of the crankshaft. This fitting cracked and the engine would not start at all.

To change this item the engine had to be removed from the aircraft and then the auxiliary gearbox had to be removed from the engine. A spare had to be sourced from another engine and then removed before fitting into Black 6. The whole process took the best part of a month and all because the torque setting was wrong due to lack of information.

The original fuel tank on Black 6 had a leak that activated the self-sealing gel, causing the capacity of the fuel tank to shrink from 400 litres to around 360 litres, which meant we needed a replacement tank that had to be manufactured.

When the fateful day of 12 October 1997 dawned, Black 6 was scheduled to make a farewell public display at Duxford. The aircraft was taken aloft by a pilot who was caught out by the difficulties in flying and particularly landing the Bf109. In the resulting crash landing the aircraft ended up on its back, across the road from the airfield, badly damaged. The pilot survived and fortunately the wreck was subsequently recovered complete. Thankfully, the decision was eventually made to rebuild this historic aircraft.

A new phase of restoration work began early in 1999, but this time with no intention to make the aircraft airworthy again. Instead it was to become a permanent museum exhibit. Many members of the team who had collaborated on Black 6's restoration to flying condition subsequently came together again to help rebuild the aircraft, including Paul Blackah, the co-author of this book. The work was completed in 2001 and the aircraft was later transferred to the RAF Museum in Hendon, north London, where it remains on display to this day.

ABOVE: An overhead view of Black 6, clearly showing the MG17 machine gun ports and the supercharger intake complete with filter assembly. *Richard Paver*

LEFT: Rubber fuel tanks. On the right is the original self-sealing tank; the other is a brand new composite unit. The tanks hold 400 litres of fuel. *Black 6 Team*

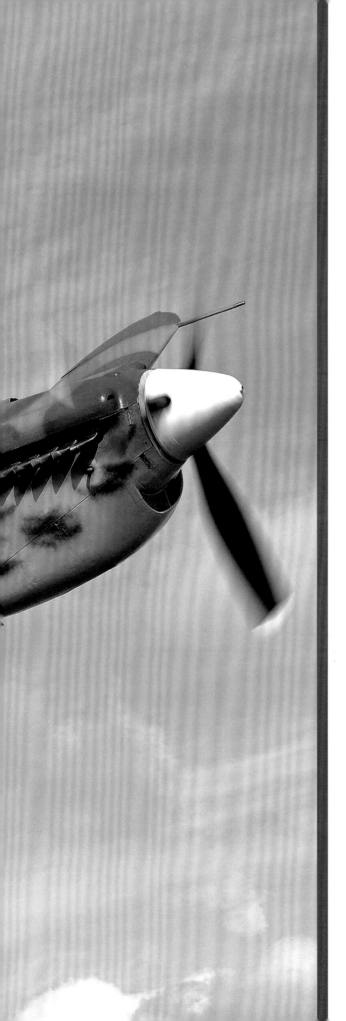

Chapter Four

The Owner's View

For those who wish to own a genuine Bf109 and make it airworthy, there are not all that many possibilities. Nevertheless, with the right money (a very large amount would be useful), and the good fortune to find an airframe in a lake or other such location, the very remote possibility of achieving the accolade of adding to the world's limited stock of airworthy 109s still exists.

LEFT: Tom Blair's Buchón Red 1, G-BWUE. The Buchón is powered by a Rolls-Royce Merlin engine which gives the fighter its distinctive appearance when compared with a genuine Bf109. *Richard Paver*

RIGHT: Aircraft serial number (Werk Nummer) plate. *All images on this page Black 6 Team*

RIGHT: Typical component data plates.

RIGHT: Aircraft build data plate.

RIGHT: The view inside the rear fuselage hatch, showing the manufacturer's plate where the 'F' has been crossed out and replaced by a 'G'.

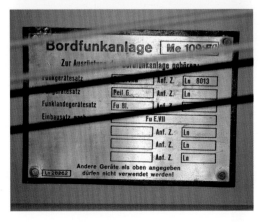

Acquiring a Bf109

Sourcing an original 109 that needs restoration would be difficult, but not impossible. If you managed to source a project, and there are still some wrecks being salvaged in Russia, it would be possible to restore the aircraft as long as you had the money. The alternative to an original 109 would be to find a Buchón airframe and consider re-engining it to resemble a 109. It would look like a 109, fly like a 109, but would not have the provenance that makes it an original 109.

After you have sourced your project, verifying its origin should be easy, providing the data plates are still fitted to major components. These data plates should have the part number and aircraft serial number stamped on them. For example, the data plates for Black 6 read BF109G2 and the aircraft serial number is 10639.

On other components, such as engine cowlings, the aircraft's serial number would be stamped. On Black 6 the engine cowlings had the serial number 10639, which corresponded with the original manufacturer's plate, which was still in place on the rear fuselage.

General expenses

Operating your Bf109 is not going to be cheap. One of the major expenses will be insurance, which will depend on the authenticity of your aircraft. A Buchón renovated and restored to flying condition would cost approximately £20–25,000 per year to insure. However, an authentic, flying Bf109 would cost nearer £55,000 per annum, due to the rarity.

At the time of writing, oil is approximately £6.50 per litre and the DB605 motor can burn up to 11 litres per hour. Fuel is approximately £1.20 per litre and the tank holds 400 litres, which will give a flying time of approximately 1 hour 45 minutes, depending on factors such as flying conditions and speed.

Although original tyres are no longer available, BAC Canberra nose tyres will do the job and fit the original wheels at a cost of approximately £400 each.

Replacement propeller blades would cost approximately £4–5,000, however these would not be original metal blades, but would be a wooden composite replacement.

Pitfalls to avoid

The main consideration on purchasing a restoration project is whether you have the facilities to house your aircraft and, if renting hangar space, whether this will be available for the duration of the project.

Financial matters are important, as in any major project, and sufficient funds should be available should any unexpected expenses arise, such as the spars on your wings being beyond saving and in need total replacement or having to have a component such as an engine bearer recast.

It is important to make sure you have all the relevant manuals and drawings, if they are available, and sourcing these *is* possible, but difficult.

Safety first

Even when the aircraft is on the ground it can kill you if not treated with respect.

1. A static propeller should always be treated as 'live' and even with the mag switch in the OFF position, it may continue to rotate after being hand turned, especially when the engine is hot.
2. Care should be taken when operating the flying controls, to ensure that there is no ground equipment or personnel around the immediate area. Being hit by an aileron would not only damage a person, but ruin the aileron as it is fabric covered.
3. Ear protection is essential when the engine is running, as prolonged exposure to engine noise can cause your hearing to deteriorate over a period of time.
4. Correct clothing should be worn at all times, eg: a set of overalls, and no ties or jewellery should be worn as they could become caught and cause injury.
5. When replenishing fluids, care should be taken that the correct fluid is put into the right reservoir, or you risk contaminating the whole system. There are so many lubricants and fluids that are packaged in similar containers that mistakes can happen if care is not taken.
6. When entering the cockpit, pockets should be emptied to prevent FOD (foreign object damage); something as small as a coin or a pen top could jam the controls with possible fatal consequences if it happened in flight.

Case History 1

Black 6 – Russ Snadden

Russ Snadden is an ex-RAF and Britannia Airways pilot. He has a passion for historic aircraft and was instrumental in getting Black 6 airworthy. He is currently working on his own project, which is a Bücker Bestmann. Although he was not the owner of Black 6 during the time that he was restoring the aircraft (or indeed at any other time), his words regarding the long restoration process give an interesting insight into the trials and tribulations of returning a valuable historic aircraft to flying condition.

For anyone with an interest in military aviation of the Second World War, owning an aircraft from that era must be top of the wish-list. Few are fortunate enough to able to convert wish to reality, however. In the late 1960s, as a young pilot in the Royal Air Force, it was painfully obvious that it was highly unlikely that I would be one of the few, but, nevertheless, my fascination with old aircraft did not diminish. As it happened, my station, Royal Air Force Gaydon, Warwickshire, was home to several historic machines including a rare Messerschmitt Me262 jet fighter and I sought permission to perform some cosmetic restoration on it. This resulted in months of spare-time work plus many hours during the working week when I was not required to fly. I can still vividly recall applying paint at 2 o'clock in the morning knowing that I would be in the air at 9am, but in those days five hours of sleep sufficed. Two years later, following posting, I determined to continue restoration work and began a search for a likely candidate.

I was (and still am) particularly interested in German aircraft. Relatively few survived post-war scrapping and these were generally in a pretty neglected and dilapidated condition. I felt they deserved better. Also, almost all of them bore inappropriate markings and I was intrigued by the possibility that their true colours lay underneath. Uncovering these, despite the time required so to do, is a fascination for me. Such work was recently described by a friend of mine as 'aircheology'. I might add that he could not understand why I would want to do such work although he admired my patience.

My preliminary investigation pinpointed a Messerschmitt Me163 a few miles distant at RAF Colerne, but the station commander refused to allow it to be moved. Approaches to the Ministry of Defence and the Imperial War Museum to permit restoration of Focke-Wulf Fw190 aircraft were similarly rebuffed and I began to wonder if I should bother. But then I targeted a Messerschmitt Bf109G, which lay neglected at RAF Wattisham, Suffolk and, with the help of the late Jack Bruce of the RAF Museum, I was able to extract it from a rather reluctant station commander. My boss had agreed to the use of a corner of our hangar, but apart from that I was very much on my own. Shortly after the arrival of the dismembered fighter, though, interest was shown by several members of the engineering side of my squadron and I soon had all the help I needed to advance my project. I rarely found myself without such hands-on support throughout the years that followed, but there is no doubt that, without the commitment of John Dixon, Paul Blackah and the late Ian Mason, and their comradeship, the aircraft which proved to be Black 6 would not have been restored.

The aim was to accurately restore the old bird and that accuracy would apply to all detail, even the type of fastener employed. It was impossible to predict the timescale of the project as all our work had to be undertaken after hours (generally) and at weekends. Besides, as the aircraft had been stripped internally, I was also faced with the very real problem of finding replacement parts. With an open cheque book this would have been much easier although not as easy as decades later, paradoxically. However, it was stipulated by the Ministry of Defence that no funding would be made available to me and this left me with no option other than to beg for parts, once located, and for help with the repair or manufacture of others. Suffice to say, some companies provided exemplary support. Others – and there were many of them – did not. Indeed, some did not even acknowledge my letter. The primary aim of our work was to restore the Bf109, but it had also been made clear from the very beginning that I would also endeavour to make it airworthy; had we found any major problem, this idea would have been dropped.

Moving from RAF Lyneham to Northolt on posting and taking the 109 with me caused a long interruption in the work. Inevitably, this move caused the loss of some of the team, but they were very quickly replaced by fresh faces. As I reflect on these days, I am always amazed at my good fortune in finding such vital support. In a leaking, unheated Nissen hut at Northolt, the old bird began to take shape. Every little part received attention and subsequent paint and, after several years, the aircraft was regaining its form. About then, however, I learned that a high-ranking officer had visited in our absence. Being unannounced, I found this most worrying. Shortly afterwards I was contacted by an engineering officer of the Battle of Britain Memorial Flight who blithely

RIGHT: The cockpit of Black 6 prior to restoration.
Black 6 Team

announced that he planned to take over the project. I doubt anyone will be surprised that I told him where to go. I gathered backing from all the senior figures I could muster and the 'abduction' was thwarted. But our days at Northolt were numbered. I was summoned to the station commander's office and given my marching orders; the aircraft was to be removed within three weeks. I was dumbfounded. Bearing in mind that the fighter was not mine (unfortunately), but in the 'care' of the Ministry of Defence, it was unbelievable that it was to be removed while being offered no alternative accommodation. Space was subsequently provided by a sympathetic engineering officer at RAF Benson where more new faces joined the team and the restoration then gathered pace.

Finally, after more years of unrelenting and seemingly non-ending graft, we found ourselves facing engine-running and a first flight. I had stipulated at the beginning that I would only undertake the restoration provided no-one looked over my shoulder; I would not tolerate interference. I think officialdom steered clear because it believed that we would fail in our task. With the Messerschmitt approaching completion, however, I discovered that senior engineering officers had visited the aircraft, again unannounced, and were seen closely inspecting the aircraft. Following some

ABOVE: Black 6 at RAF Benson.
Black 6 Team

vociferous protest, I was asked to attend a meeting in Whitehall where the future was discussed. Some time later I was informed that the aircraft would be allowed to fly, albeit under a civil ticket and not a military one as I had hoped. Good news, we thought, but then we were told that Duxford, Cambridgeshire, would be its future home and that it would be allocated to one of the private companies there and flown under the auspices of the Imperial War Museum. Could we arrange a handover?

Duxford did become its home, but only after the 'brass' relented and we retained our hold on

BELOW: At RAF Benson with the engine just installed.
Black 6 Team

the aircraft. This compromise was reached after months of wrangling and ill-feeling. The fact that such a decision was taken without involving the people performing the restoration was a clear indication of the autocratic attitude of those in power at the time. It was but a foretaste.

So, we completed the reconstruction at Benson and asked the Civil Aviation Authority to inspect our baby with a view to issuing a Permit to Test. We dreaded the inspectors' visit as they were a completely unknown quantity. After an extensive examination of the aircraft, I was told that the Permit was approved. Not only that, we were complimented on the standard of our work. It was an amazing day!

Prior to flight, the Daimler-Benz DB605A engine had first to be brought to life. This motor had been completely overhauled by enthusiasts within the Rolls-Royce company at Filton who had overcome many, many problems on the way. Engine-testing was accomplished by one of their number and we found ourselves anticipating a first flight. But who would fly it? I realised that, left to his own devices, the relevant officer in Whitehall would inform me who he had selected so I stuck my oar in, so to speak, and suggested Group Captain Reg Hallam. Reg was a highly-experienced test pilot and also had experience of the Hispano HA-1112, a Spanish-built version of the Bf109 but with considerable differences, including the powerplant. Reg accepted my invitation with some alacrity and, on the 17th March 1991, just short of 19 years since I received it, he lifted the aircraft into grey skies over Benson. It was a lovely sight although there was a great deal of apprehension attendant, of course. Reg was impressed by the aircraft but he experienced difficulty in keeping straight during the take-off run, not helped by the poor condition of the grass and wet and windy conditions. The propeller struck the ground in the process and had to be repaired following the flight. Nevertheless, the 109 was undoubtedly very fast, even with a bent airscrew.

Some weeks later, Black 6 flew from Benson for the last time to its new home near Cambridge and flight-testing was completed successfully. The Imperial War Museum was already planning future displays and, as we would require several pilots to accomplish

future programmes, these had to be found. Reg Hallam had decided to resign his commission and, in so doing, removed himself from the list of pilots as it had been decreed that all pilots must be Royal Air Force, bar one, that is, but I won't dwell on that. Before he left us, he selected Squadron Leader Dave Southwood, a fellow test pilot and, for the team, a particularly happy choice. Watching the fighter being displayed by Dave was a delight to us all and his evident enthusiasm for the machine only heightened that pleasure. It was almost as if it had been made for him. Later, Flight Lieutenant Charlie Brown joined the ranks and went on to log more hours than the others in the flying team.

IWM accepted bookings for displays and my team performed maintenance and provided the required support. 'Away' events spread us very thinly as people were needed both at Duxford and the venue. We attended displays in Paris and Jersey, for example, both of which required a good deal of planning. Paris was within the fuel range of the Messerschmitt, but as the transit flight to Jersey entailed flying towards the Dover area in order to cross the Channel at its narrowest point and then due west along the north coast of France, a fuel-stop was required to allow the aircraft to arrive over Jersey with acceptable reserve fuel. So we needed a send-off party at Duxford, more team members at the refuel airfield and a small group at Jersey. It was very hard on the team, especially when occasionally things went wrong. The aircraft was very well received everywhere we went and was usually the star of the show. Afterwards, it was flown home where, if we had anyone available, it would be put in a hangar, cleaned and inspected. Although we had a few small problems away from base, it is fair to say that, the more we flew, the greater became our understanding of our charge and the more serviceable it became. Having a small team dedicated to this one machine ensured the very best care and we, in turn, were very proud of Black 6.

Over winter the engine was inhibited and in-depth maintenance was undertaken. The Daimler-Benz caused us many headaches in the first two seasons particularly with valve and piston-ring problems and we were forced to cancel large portions of several display seasons to rectify the faults. We also had a new fuel tank made following leaks in the original unit and this caused us to miss most of one season. Consequently, IWM persuaded the Ministry of Defence that the period of the loan be extended beyond the agreed three years. By 1997, however, we were very aware that it was likely that the 109 would be removed from our care. IWM, in an effort to retain it at Duxford, evolved a plan whereby it would continue limited flying and only at Duxford. At no time was I ever contacted by the Ministry of Defence to inform me of its plans, nor, it should be said was any information forthcoming from IWM. Evidently my team and I were of no import. So, as the last show of the 1997 season approached, we were very apprehensive as rumours abounded that it was to be our last. There is no doubt that IWM knew, of course, as a press showing of Black 6 was arranged two days before the display for no obvious reason. I am convinced that the chief pilot also knew as he pencilled himself in for the planned last display of the show. On that fateful day he mishandled the coolant system causing an engine overheat which led to a hasty return to terra firma and a turnover in a ploughed field adjacent to the airfield. Fortunately I was not present as I had been rostered to fly for my company; I learned about the crash upon my return home.

The following day we inspected our baby, which lay, inverted, on a farm trailer with rainwater pouring from every orifice. Damage to the rear fuselage and vertical tail was severe but the closer we looked the more we realised that it was localised. 'It's repairable,' said Ian Mason. What a lovely speech! Discussions then took place about the way forward, but without our input. No one thought to solicit information or advice from the team. We were ignored, yet again. However, as it was required that the aircraft be returned to the Ministry of Defence in good order, we anticipated – *expected* – to be asked to begin the rebuild but, no, the rules demanded that such work be put out to tender and we were forbidden from touching the aircraft for almost a year while the bureaucrats dealt with procedure. Salt in an already-festering wound. It was apparent that no thought whatsoever was given to the fact that my team

and I knew the aircraft in intimate detail and that only we could *properly* restore it. After some debate, and with considerable distaste, we decided to tender for the work. To do so, I had to form a limited company but, thankfully, our bid was successful and we began the work that should have started months before.

Damage was confined, in the main, to the rear fuselage and vertical tail, but the propeller and its spinner were destroyed and the cockpit canopy damaged. We removed every component from the fuselage before setting about cutting out the damaged areas. A new section of rear fuselage was grafted in using a jig and an original, but reskinned, fin fitted and the rudder rebuilt using as much original material as possible. While these repairs were being effected, the team cleaned up all the internal equipment and repainted where necessary. I might add that this work was not required by contract. Simultaneously our engine 'bods' partially stripped the engine for inspection as required by the Air Accident Investigation Branch as part of its thorough investigation. Nothing was found which could have contributed to events during that last flight. The Daimler-Benz was assembled and inhibited, after which the exhaust ports and supercharger intake were sealed. The original VDM propeller, which we had held in reserve, was assembled and fitted together with a replacement spinner supplied by a good friend in Germany. Our final task at Duxford was to repaint the aeroplane, a task with which we were very familiar. I must say that it looked beautiful when all the masking materials were removed. Prior to the required move to the RAF Museum, Hendon, we learned that a representative had first to examine the machine. I was told that, when asked what he was looking for, he replied that he was checking, among other things, that there were no holes where equipment should be. His questioner retorted that he was b****y lucky that *anything* was there, given the condition it was in before the team started work.

The old bird is now to be found in the Milestones of Flight Hall at Hendon, by a strange coincidence close to the Me262 upon which I had previously worked. Since its installation I have visited it but twice, on both occasions to fit further items of equipment in the cockpit. I am proud – as proud as any owner could possibly be – of what we achieved through our long, voluntary effort. As a result of an association covering 30 years, the last genuine combat aircraft of the Luftwaffe to fly is now painstakingly restored and in its original colours – Bf109G-2, Black 6 of 8./JG 77. I must confess to some sadness. Its second career was incredibly short, covering only three and a half display seasons, scant reward for many years of hard work. However, it serves to illustrate what can be achieved by a small, dedicated group. I thank them all from the bottom of my heart.

Case History 2

Owning and flying a Buchón: Cliff Spink

Pilot and warbird owner Cliff Spink describes some of the joys of owning and flying a Hispano Buchón, having also flown Black 6.

If there is one aircraft that gets the pulse beating a bit faster in a warbird pilot it is the Bf109 – or its close cousin the Buchón. During the Second World War Adolf Hitler gave 25 Bf109G airframes to the Spanish Government of Franco – a closet Nazi despite Spain's neutrality. Unfortunately there were no engines and the airframes languished until after the war when Hispano picked up the project, produced a lot more airframes, and fitted Rolls-Royce Merlins, thanks to the improvement in relations between Britain and Spain.

The result was the Buchón, which was the first main fighter back in the resurgent Spanish Air Force and it went on to see active service in the then Spanish Sahara. The swansong for the Buchón was in 1968 when a squadron of Buchóns, flown by mainly Spanish pilots (with a few US Confederate Air Force), flew in the *Battle of Britain* film – our Buchón took on the mantle of 'Red 7' in the film.

The first 109 I was lucky enough to fly was the 109G Black 6, which I flew for two seasons. The Buchón, being a Gustav airframe, displays most if not all of the handling characteristics of its parent although from a personal point of view

I feel much happier sitting behind a Merlin. The DB605 was undoubtedly a good engine but, being an inverted 'V', and bigger cubic capacity, it took careful management and was prone to plug fouling quite quickly – which is why it had a specific system for plug cleaning. And frankly, at the lower levels that we fly, I could never detect a difference in power. I sometimes get a bit irritated by 'experts' who say that the Buchón is not a real 109, *it is*, and it was developed in much the same way as other aircraft that had different power plants put in them as they went through their operational life. At a recent air show in the Buchón, I was flying with an old friend from Germany who was also flying a Buchón which had been refitted with a DB605. His problems – overheating and general engine handling – were so much more than mine, and he said with some passion 'Oh for a Merlin' – and he meant it. The first thing that is apparent about the 109 is that is actually quite small – just see it sitting beside, say, a Mustang and you get the picture. It looks mean and purposeful – aggressive – and that is a pretty good indicator of the way it is going to handle. Small wings and a big engine also mean speed, and it is fast, but what you gain in straight line performance you lose in turning ability, and the automatic slats give the clue that the 109 needs watching at slow speed.

The cockpit is small – too small for some pilots of today's generation – and creature comforts are few. The seat needs adjusting before flight – no handy raise/lower lever like the Spitfire – and the rudder bars have no pilot adjustment. A 'hard hat' is out of the question as the canopy sits almost on my cranium so a noise-cancelling soft headset must suffice.

With the canopy closed and locked (it is very heavy) the pre-start checks are completed – elevator trim and flap are two large wheels by your left thigh which can be moved together when required and I always set to the take-off positions at this stage. Throttle and prop controls are conventional as is the throttle friction – mixture is automatic so idle cut off is a 'pull' bar on the top left of the main instrument panel. Instruments are a bit of a mix but have a German influence – airspeed in knots, but engine manifold in atmospheres for example. Main fuel cock is hidden down towards your right ankle and is rotated and pulled out to turn on – this is also an oil cock and therefore has particular significance. Electrical switches are all ganged on the right cockpit wall and are pretty logical – once engine pre-oil is complete I switch on the boost pump for about '4 potatoes' to get fuel in the lines and to the carb. The primer is identical to that in a Griffon Spitfire and two shots are more than enough for a cold start – throttle set about ½in open, 'clear prop?', mag switch to both on, and, with toe brakes firmly on, press the boost coil and start buttons together. The Merlin 500 is an excellent starter and roars into life and an immediate check of engine oil pressure is followed by hydraulic pressure check and ensure that rad flaps have stayed fully open. The cooling radiator flaps are hydraulic and controlled by a 'T' bar on the main instrument panel which selects fully open or closed or, by putting the bar horizontal, keeps the rads at an intermediate position.

The 109 is very tail heavy on the ground and needs plenty of power to get the tail weaving even with the tail wheel unlocked – the view forward is awful. Warm up is unremarkable – the radiators are effective on the Buchón and the oil temp comes up nicely without the coolant temp running away. The run-up can be made at higher boost/rpm than on a Spitfire because the tail stays firmly down – not that uneasy sensation of the tail getting light. Final checks – I go left to right again which is my technique, but I am sure the normal pneumonic would work. The flaps are at 15°, tail trim one degree up (there is no rudder trim), throttle friction tight, canopy closed and locked, instruments erect and set, engine T's and P's all OK, hydraulic pressure up, fuel boost pump on, fuel cock on, harness and a flying controls check. I always run through a final 'Captain's Brief' to myself – just running through a review of my actions in the event of minor or major failure during the take-off sequence.

All operations in 'Black 6' were from the grass, but since those times I have operated Buchón successfully from hard runways. In fact, rocking and rolling on poor grass runways on take-off, before adequate aileron control is achieved, can be much more demanding than the smooth progression on tarmac – although crosswind must be a consideration.

Line up today is on Duxford grass runway, a little off runway heading so that the full runway can be seen right up to the application of take-off power, and a final check 'Tail wheel locked'. Smoothly up on the power – no rush – and start working at keeping the aircraft absolutely straight with that appallingly small rudder. Don't get the tail up too quickly – you could have the ride of a lifetime if you do – and get right aileron in to counter the natural and significant tendency for 'dig in' to the left from engine torque. Take-off is an all-action event, but the addition of the modified disc brakes has helped – a quick dab to straighten the nose at the slower speeds is now possible. The take-off run is not overlong, but it is not an aircraft for 'exotic' departures – just let it accelerate, which it does quite quickly, and hit the red up button on the gear which cycles at a modest pace. Ease the throttle to climb power and drop the rpm to 2,400, rads closed, flaps up and trim.

With no rudder trim, during acceleration/deceleration and power/prop change, the aircraft needs constant attention with rudder, but that said I have flown a lot worse. It trims well in pitch – the trim moves the whole tail surface – and it is quite firm and stable in the cruise. For the same power setting it is faster than the Merlin Spitfires in the cruise, but it does not have nearly the harmonisation in the controls – mind you what has? It is heavy in pitch, but it has a very good roll rate for this type of aircraft – four point rolls are crisp and a delight to execute. During an aerobatic sequence you work hard as it feels quite heavy to haul about, it is a physical exercise. It is most important to keep the aircraft in balance as it will roll into a hard turn and drop its nose if the ball is not in the middle – a bit disconcerting at low level. Looping is OK, but I tend to restrict my looping manoeuvres to the half-Cuban – as the nose comes down below the horizon the roll out can be precise. Energy management is important in any aircraft doing low-level aeros, but none more so than in the Buchón. A safe, elegant and reasonably tight display can be achieved as long as energy is kept high.

Even during warm days I have not had to crack open the rad flaps during a display, but before I run in for the final break to land I put them open in good time – with quite a

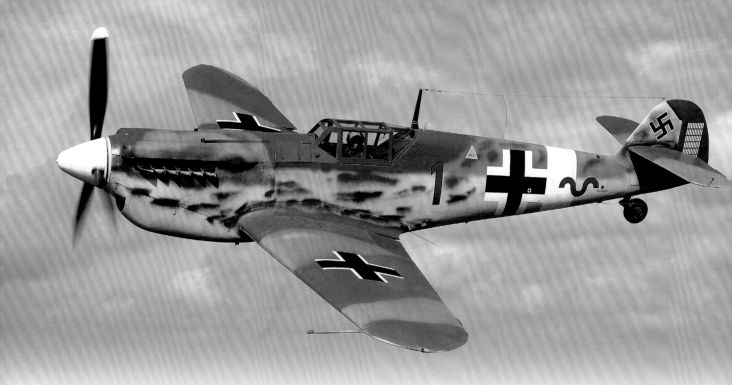

ABOVE: Buchón
**G-BWUE was restored
by the Real Aircraft
Company (RAC) and
is now owned and
operated by Spitfire Ltd
at Duxford.** *Richard Paver*

BELOW: **An overhead
view of G-BWUE. The
blisters on the wings
are to allow the wheels,
which are fitted with
larger tyres, to fit into
the undercarriage bays.**
Richard Paver

significant airbrake effect – and cool the engine
down. Fuel boost pump goes on for landing (it
is probably on from my display anyway), about
2,400 on the rpm and then I set up for the run
and break. There is a lot to do downwind so
giving yourself a short downwind leg is not a
good idea. Speed OK and hit the green u/c
down button and check the gear is moving,
then it is pretty constant winding back on the
flap and tailplane trim to get full flap down by
the end of the downwind leg. Although I am
looking to have full flap down as I start to turn
finals there have been occasions when I have
been still been winding in the turn. The u/c
greens do have bulb failure sometimes, but
there are mechanical indicators which are the

primary indication and that vital check that
the tail wheel is locked. Start the finals turn
at 100kt, gradually easing to 90kt as wings
come level and 85kt across the hedge – slats
are firmly out all the way round. The Buchón is
very speed stable around finals. With prop fully
forward and power set it comes round on rails,
but it does not feel at all comfortable turning
tight in this regime or with power back in a
'glide' – better to take an early go around rather
than persevering with something that is less
than in the groove.

The landing is achieved on three points
and the aircraft sits down quite well – contrary
to popular thinking – but the fun can start a
split second after arrival! It will swing and the
direction can be unpredictable, but immediate
and significant input from the rudder will
keep her straight, at least initially. Rudder
effectiveness falls off quickly with speed decay
and this is where the new brakes have been a
godsend. In other 109 types I have flown the
brakes have been pretty average with all the
problems of fade etc., but these are progressive
and give you the ability to just bring the nose
straight at the slower speeds when the rudder
has become mere decoration.

I don't think that I am a masochist but I really
enjoy flying the Buchón. It will never replace
the Spitfire in my affections, but it is very high
on the list of vintage aircraft that I have been
privileged to fly. All heat and fire and a challenge
to fly well – an ideal warbird then.

Case History 3

Teutonic threesome: German-owned Buchóns

There are three airworthy, or, more accurately, potentially airworthy Bf109 lookalikes in Germany. All three are effectively not genuine Bf109s, with two of them being Hispano Buchóns re-engined with Daimler-Benz DB605 engines, while the third is basically a Buchón but with some genuine Bf109 components and again re-engined with DB605 power. Unfortunately two of these aircraft were involved in accidents during 2008, one of these mishaps, which took place in full public view at the Berlin Air Show ILA 2008, being the result of the Bf109's long-standing tendency to bite its pilots either on landing or take-off.

The ownership of these three aircraft brings to light some interesting facets of the display of aircraft from the former Nazi era in Germany. The flying of the genuine Bf109G-2 Black 6 in Britain was universally accepted as the display of a genuine war veteran, which was fully worthy of the interest and often reverence that was shown towards it, despite it having been on the German side and having flown in combat against British and Commonwealth forces during its brief wartime activity in North Africa during the Second World War. In Germany, however, this situation is somewhat different, and the status of the three airworthy Bf109 lookalikes is usually consciously shrouded in as much ambiguity as possible, particularly to foreign media and aviation correspondents who ask after them.

The three aircraft are part of the Willy Messerschmitt Stiftung (*Stiftung* meaning Foundation), which is an organisation that exists to keep alive the memory of and to celebrate the undoubted achievements of Willy Messerschmitt. It is supported by EADS, which is the multi-national European Aeronautic, Defence and Space Company. This large grouping of many national aerospace companies is the home of such important current programmes as Airbus and Eurofighter, and is a massive aerospace player on the world market. EADS supports the Messerschmitt Stiftung in a number of practical

ways, something that those of us who actively support aircraft restoration find no problem with whatsoever. On the other hand, EADS does not actively talk about this support, and some of its employees do not even admit to its existence. This is presumably because it would not wish to be associated with some of the blacker periods in recent German history, even though the successors to some of the wartime German aircraft companies are present in its latter-day line-up. This is understandable, but no one in their right mind would find a problem with a well-financed consortium like EADS actively supporting historic aircraft preservation – indeed there are many in the current 'warbird' community who would welcome that kind of active support. Even so, EADS very often shows unease about being associated with these aircraft, and the Messerschmitt Stiftung maintains a very detached air except to some elements of the German media.

Perhaps there will come a time when the Germans are prepared, or at least comfortable, to be more open about the status of these aircraft, particularly to sources outside Germany, but it obviously remains a difficult subject for some. Nevertheless, many of us take our hats off to EADS for providing support to the Messerschmitt Stiftung, and to the Foundation itself, for keeping three Bf109 lookalikes in the air, barring accidents.

ABOVE: Bearing the titles 'EADS' and 'Messerschmitt Stiftung' on its fuselage side, the Bf109G-10/Buchón composite, D-FDME, Black 2, prepares for take-off at the Berlin Air Show ILA 2008 in May 2008. It is one of three Bf109G look-alikes that the Messerschmitt Stiftung looks after at Manching in Germany in conjunction with the aerospace giant EADS, the whole operation being shrouded in as much ambiguity as possible. *Messe-Berlin*

Chapter Five

The Pilot's View

The Bf109 is not an easy aircraft to fly. Or rather, it is not an easy aircraft to take-off and land. The type's narrow-track main undercarriage was a problem at the time when the Bf109 was in front-line service, and has remained so ever since. It is ill-advised to try to land a Bf109 on a paved surface or in a crosswind, and the aircraft is always ready to bite on take-off and landing, causing the pilot to have to hold on to a concentration and perspiration level above and beyond that required for aircraft with a much more forgiving wide-track main undercarriage.

LEFT: The narrow track of the main undercarriage of the Bf109 series is well illustrated in this view of the EADS/Messerschmitt Stiftung's airworthy Bf109G-10/Buchón composite. *Messe-Berlin*

ABOVE This pose was characteristic of many Bf109 accidents, the result of a ground-loop and undercarriage collapse. This particular aircraft is a Czech-built Avia S-99. *4+ Publishing Co*

Unfortunately, two of the currently sometimes airworthy 'Bf109s' in Germany have suffered major accidents due to the tendency of the Messerschmitt to ground-loop on landing or swing unexpectedly on take-off. The most recent of these occurred at the Berlin Air Show ILA 2008 at Berlin-Schönefeld airport, where EADS display pilot Walter Eichhorn was caught out by a sudden crosswind while attempting a paved runway landing in the former Hans Dittes

Bf109G Black 2. The resulting spectacular ground-loop took place right in front of the co-author of this book, Malcolm Lowe, who photographed the escapade and was subsequently interviewed on German television as a close eye-witness to the event.

The following eye-witness accounts and notes give an interesting look into the flying of the Bf109 from a pilot's perspective, from a diversity of piloting experiences.

The EADS/Messerschmitt Stiftung's Bf109G-10/Buchón composite came to grief during the Berlin Air Show ILA 2008 when pilot Walter Eichhorn was caught out by a sudden crosswind while attempting a paved runway landing. *Malcolm V. Lowe*

Flying the Bf109G: Dave Southwood

Dave Southwood is an ex-RAF Empire Test Pilots School pilot. As a test pilot, Dave has flown all manner of aircraft and was, therefore, an excellent candidate for piloting Black 6. He still flies historic aircraft at various displays around the country.

These notes are written largely from memory and from the checklist/notes that I used as an *aide-memoire* for flying Black 6. They relate specifically to that airframe and engine combination. Some of the procedures were developed in the light of experience gained. Undoubtedly, some of the procedures detailed here would need to be modified for other airframe/engine combinations.

Engine starting

The propeller was set to MANUAL and 12.00, the throttle was opened about 1 inch, the fuel was selected to P1+P2 and the ICO forward (run). Initially, the engine was primed for 8 strokes after pressure was felt. Immediately before the external starter crank handle was removed, the fuel pump was switched on and another 3–4 strokes given on the primer. Note that starting difficulties were not usually as a result of over-priming; it was rare to over-prime. As the external starter crank handle was removed, the mags were selected to '1+ 2', the spark plug cleaner pulled, and as the starter crew jumped off the trailing edge of wing the starter clutch was engaged. When the engine fired, the cockpit starter clutch handle was released, and the spark plug cleaner was released slowly. The throttle was adjusted to warm up at 1000–1200rpm; the warm-up was normally done with the rad flaps set to AUTO and once the oil temp was above 20°C, the aircraft was taxied.

Once the engine was running smoothly, the electric fuel pump was turned OFF. We burnt out a few with continuous running until we discovered that it should only be run for 5 minutes per sortie (as I recall).

Taxiing

The aircraft was very tail heavy and there were no worries about tipping on to the nose. All taxiing was done with the tailwheel unlocked. In order to turn tightly, full forward stick was applied (to unload the tailwheel), a 'handful' of power applied (to give some yawing moment from the rudder and to further unload the tailwheel by increasing lift from the tailplane) and full brake applied in the required direction of turn. Once the tailwheel had broken out of the detent, it was easy to control the turn using brake alone. It was easy to stop the turn by applying brake opposite to the direction of turn. The tailwheel quickly dropped into the detent, and subsequent small, gradual heading changes could be made by brake alone. Note that tight turns on grass, especially if wet, often resulted in the wheel skidding along the ground and the aircraft not turning. However, one man holding back on the wing tip could generate enough moment to cause the tailwheel to 'break out' of the detent and then the turn was continued easily. Obviously, the amount of power needed to taxi determined how much you needed to warm up the engine prior to moving.

Run-up

The minimum temperatures prior to run-up were 70°C coolant and 20°C oil. The rad flaps had opened fully by the time the run-up was commenced. The oil pressure was checked at 3.5–8atm. The mags were checked at 2000rpm and the max drop was 50rpm. If the mag drop was excessive, the spark plug cleaner was pulled out for about 20 secs (I think – it may have been shorter). The rpm dropped to about 1400 (I think) and the engine ran somewhat roughly, but it recovered immediately on letting the spark plug cleaner in. However, this hardly ever needed to be done.

It was also recommended that the fuel supply was checked by running at 2000rpm on P1 then on P2 for 30 secs each. However, this really increased the coolant temp on a hot day so I selected P1 as I started taxiing and after about 2 minutes selected P2 for about 2 minutes. I always did the run up on P1+P2 *and checked that it was gated* as it was easy to forget to reset this before take-off. The importance of this check was that the engine was run on each fuel supply for long enough such that it was not just running on fuel remaining in the supply line that had been deselected.

Take-off

The coolant temperature rose quickly after start. At best, you would get about 12 minutes from start to reaching the coolant temp limit of 110°C (cold day, first start of the day). At worst it was only 6–7 minutes (hot day, start up within 1 hour of shutdown from a previous sortie).

In the pre-take-off checks, I set 20° flap and 1° nose up tailplane trim. The original data said 0° trim, but 1° nose up was added after the propeller ground strike on the first sortie. (Frankly, it made no difference.) The prop was checked at MANUAL and 12.00 as I did not risk the automatic system malfunctioning during such a critical flight phase. (So saying, we never had any malfunctions with the AUTO RPM control.) The biggest scope for errors in the pre take-off checks were not selecting the mags to 1+2, not checking the fuel was GATED at P1+P2, and not selecting the electric fuel pump ON (although this was just as a back-up in case of engine driven pump failure – it was not necessary to get take-off power). *NOTE: Our crosswind component limit for take-off and landing was 10kt. We did not accept a tailwind component for take-off (unless the total wind speed was less than 5kt when a 1–2kt tailwind component might be accepted on a long runway). WE ONLY FLEW FROM GRASS RUNWAYS.*

Once lined up on the runway the tailwheel was locked while rolling forward slowly (1–2kt). IT WAS ABSOLUTELY ESSENTIAL TO LOCK THE TAILWHEEL FOR TAKE-OFF. Power was increased slowly to 1.1atm with the tailwheel still on the ground. With the MAP set and the aircraft running straight, the tail was raised SLOWLY until just clear of the ground then the pitch attitude held. Raising the tail too quickly or too high gave a marked swing to the left. Generally, the right rudder force needed during the take-off roll was moderate and easy to apply, equating to about half rudder deflection. Sometimes, a rapid yaw occurred (usually to the left), possibly as a result of a bump on the runway, a gust of wind or, more usually, a too rapid throttle movement. This yaw could be stopped with a rapid rudder input of up to full deflection; brake was rarely needed but it always was considered as an option. NO ATTEMPT WAS MADE TO CORRECT BACK TO RUNWAY HEADING; the heading achieved when the yaw was contained was maintained. Any attempt to yaw back to runway heading led to the aircraft rolling opposite to the direction of yaw and the potential for a high-speed ground loop was marked. Neutral aileron was maintained throughout the take-off roll. Once stabilised on the main wheels in a tail low attitude, a small back pressure was applied to the stick until the aircraft became airborne, often with some small bounces on the main wheels if the take-off speed was low.

Initial climb

When positively airborne (i.e. no skipping on the main wheels and a positive rate of climb), the brakes were selected on then off and the undercarriage UP button pressed in. The MAP was checked at 1.1atm, the propeller set to AUTO and the RPM monitored to check a reduction to about 2200. Power was then set to 1.15atm/2,300rpm for the climb. Any failure for the propeller to govern correctly on selecting AUTO would have needed an immediate reselection of MANUAL and a blade pitch of 11.30 to be set, although this problem never occurred. (Before the AUTO function was set up such that it could be used, after take-off an initial blade angle of 11.30 worked well.) WARNING: If the propeller blade angle was kept at 12.00 in MANUAL, an RPM overspeed occurred very soon after take-off and certainly well before the climb speed of 270kmh (168mph). Once the engine was set up as above, the flaps were retracted. The remaining two actions were easily forgotten; pulling the undercarriage UP button out once the undercarriage had locked UP (red lights on) to stop the hydraulic pump running, and selecting the electric fuel pump OFF. The coolant temperature, if high, dropped fairly quickly once settled in the climb.

Cruise

Radiator flaps If the rad flaps were kept in AUTO, they maintained a coolant temp of around 85°C. The rad flaps were then fairly wide open which generated a significant amount of drag. Once stabilised in the climb/cruise I adjusted the rad flaps manually to maintain 90–95°C (min 70°C, max 115°C), which gave significantly less drag. On a cool day with cruise power set (1.0atm, 2,000rpm) the rad flaps were fully closed. With display power set (1.15atm, 2,300rpm) they were normally set to be open about 2–3 inches at the trailing edge. WARNING: If operating the rad flaps manually, a close scan of coolant temperature was necessary, as they had to be adjusted periodically to maintain the desired coolant temperature. If drag was not critical, the rad flaps were operated in AUTO.

Power setting and AUTO RPM set-up

The AUTO RPM was set up so that it governed correctly to the optimum running line at the continuous power setting (1.15atm, 2,300rpm). Any small errors away from this power were accepted. Nominal cruise power was 1.0atm, 2,000rpm. The technique for setting cruise power was to set 1.0atm with the throttle and see what rpm resulted. If it was 2000 or greater, the propeller was kept in AUTO. However, sometimes it was slightly less than 2000 (1900–1950), in which case the propeller was set to MANUAL and the blade angle adjusted to give 2050–2100. This was so that the engine was not overboosted and also to ensure that the generator stayed on line (which required a nominal 2000rpm). Note that there were no 'Low Volts' or 'Generator Warning' lights.

Trim settings

The aileron and rudder fixed trim tabs were adjusted to give centralised slip ball and wings level flight with cruise power (1.0atm, 2000rpm) set in straight and level flight. If adjustments were needed, the rudder trim had to be adjusted first before the required aileron trim tab adjustments could be made. Note that if the aileron trim was correct at these cruise conditions, it was correct throughout almost the entire required flight envelope.

Aerobatics and other manoeuvres

V_{NE} dive On air tests we flew to 650kmh (404mph) and therefore the V_{NE} on the Permit to Fly was 585kmh (364mph) (90%). It was easy to achieve 650kmh (404mph) in a shallow dive and to exceed it would have been easy. I think that the power setting for this test was 1.3atm, 2,600rpm. The speeds that we flew to were more than adequate for all displays and film work that we did. In the Buchón that I flew (the ex-Charles Church machine) a limitation had been promulgated that it was not to be trimmed in pitch above 250kias (463kmh) because the high stick forces required to pull out of the dive would have resulted in a large altitude loss. In Black 6 I did not think that such a limitation was necessary.

Aerobatics For displays I set 1.15atm with the throttle set to AUTO. Before the AUTO RPM was functioning I set 1.15atm and then set the propellor blade angle to 11.05 at entry to a loop; at 420kmh (261mph) this gave 2,300rpm. Approaching the vertical (climbing) the blade angle was reset to 11.15 by reference to the gauge. Once in the vertical (diving) in a loop, or once stabilised erect on the 45° descending line in a half Cuban, the blade angle was reset to 11.05. WARNING: Looking ahead in the cockpit to reset the prop blade angle while descending during low-level aerobatics was a distraction which could lead to ground impact! Vertical manoeuvres such as loops and half Cubans were entered at a minimum speed of 420kmh (261mph) (with 450kmh/280mph minimum for an upwards quarter vertical roll) and height at the top was approximately 0.6km (c.2,000ft) above entry. Rudder forces to keep straight were moderate and easily applied. However, after the ailerons were re-covered one winter some aileron 'snatch' often occurred at the top of looping manoeuvres. This was disconcerting but did not cause a control problem. Eventually, this characteristic disappeared before its cause had been identified. There was obviously some tendency for aileron snatching associated with high angle of attack/low speed flight, possibly related to aileron covering/rigging. Another characteristic that I saw once was with an excessive amount of rudder (in the same sense as the aileron) while rolling erect during a half Cuban, a large pitch down occurred, probably due to the sideslip. This again was disconcerting, caused a large yaw and a marked increase in dive angle. I saw no signs of departure but the lesson was that only moderate rudder should be used for co-ordination during rolls at low speed.

Roll performance was standard for Second World War fighters (poor!). Full aileron was easy to apply, some rudder co-ordination was needed to keep straight and roll performance was similar in both directions. All rolls were carried out on a positive climbing line and I considered that it was quite safe to roll at low level.

Stalling Stalling characteristics were benign in both clean and landing configurations. A 'clunk' was heard as the slats deployed as angle of attack was increased but no associated roll, pitch or yaw occurred. If any sideslip was present, one slat would deploy before the other but again there were no upsets. In low-speed, wings-level stalls, just prior to the stall there was some buffet and the stall was characterised by a slight wing drop, mild pitch down and often a 'snatch' on the ailerons (I cannot remember in which direction). Recovery was straightforward by releasing stick backpressure and smoothly applying power. If power was increased too rapidly full aileron and rudder could be needed to control the torque and propwash effects. Accelerated stalls (with display power set) in turns and pulling through from low speed loops were similar and I considered that the stall warning was adequate and the stall characteristics benign enough that the stalls were not a problem or risk for low-level aerobatics.

Spinning We did not spin Black 6, and I believe that there was no need nor justification to do so. I would always argue strongly against spinning aircraft such as these.

Circuit, approach and landing

Rejoining the circuit the rad flaps were selected to AUTO and the electric fuel pump switched ON. Obviously, the tailwheel was confirmed locked. The flaps required a lot of effort and time to wind down, so this was done either during a long downwind leg or while rejoining, although the speed then had to be kept below the 250kmh limit (155mph). If the throttle was pulled back to idle with the propeller selected at AUTO, the RPM reduced excessively and the engine ran roughly (the AUTO prop function was not really worth using below 1.0atm). Therefore, before I reduced power on the break I selected the prop to MANUAL (which froze the blades at the current angle) then reduced MAP slowly while progressively increasing the prop blade angle to 11.45 (to achieve adequate hydraulic pump output to lower the undercarriage). This ensured that 2,600rpm was not exceeded. The undercarriage was selected down below the limit of 250kmh (155 mph), and once it indicated locked down, the DOWN button was pulled out (easily forgotten!). The blade angle was then reset to 11.30 (to minimise prop overspeeds during a go-around). 200kmh (124mph) was aimed for at the end of the downwind leg and maintained around the finals turn, using power as required. 200kmh (124mph) was treated as a minimum as well as a target around the finals turn, and as it was difficult to lose speed on finals it was better to go-around from a fast approach and try again. However, side-slipping was quite effective for losing excess height but the aircraft had to be stabilised at zero sideslip at a sensible height in order to get a touchdown without any drift. Long straight-in approaches were avoided; curving approaches to a low roll out was the best technique. Once rolled out, the speed was reduced using the throttle so that 175kmh (109mph) was achieved at the threshold. Field of View on the approach was reasonable and speed stability was good. It was important to trim on finals as, with the variable incidence tailplane, elevator authority for the flare was reduced if the approach was flown holding a pull force.

As the threshold was crossed the throttle was closed and the aircraft smoothly flared to keep flying for as long as possible. It floated far more than many tailwheel aircraft and it was very important to keep it flying wings level about 2ft above the ground while it decelerated. Eventually the aircraft dropped on in the three-point attitude. Often it 'bucked' around on a rough strip and it was important just to maintain the pitch attitude until it settled when the stick was held fully aft. Below touchdown speed the ailerons and rudder were ineffective and directional control on the ground needed very rapid large rudder and differential brake inputs to keep straight. Once under control the brakes were used symmetrically to slow down. They were not very powerful and it appeared to take a long time to eventually bring the aircraft to a halt. The tailwheel was unlocked once at walking speed and before attempting to turn off the runway.

The coolant temperature rose after landing and long taxi distances were not possible before the temperature limit was reached. Note that once the engine was shut down the block temperature continued to rise due to the loss of coolant flow. Therefore a shutdown at 115°C could still damage the engine.

There were several aspects to be avoided at all cost:

a. Wheeled landings The locked tailwheel was the main source of directional stability during the landing roll out. Rudder authority was insufficient for directional control at idle power with the tailwheel off the ground (or unlocked!). If during the flare the mainwheels touched before the three point attitude was achieved, I made an aft stick input to get airborne again and continued with the deceleration about 2ft above the ground to then land in the three-point attitude.

b. Reduced threshold speeds Due to the protracted float during the landing flare there was a great temptation to reduce the threshold speed below 175kmh (109mph). Any attempt to do this would probably lead to a hard landing as the normal flare would not arrest the rate of descent. I tried it only once (in a Buchón).

c. Crosswinds and tailwinds With up to a 10kt crosswind component no consideration had to be given to crosswind landing technique. If you had to think about which crosswind technique to use, the wind was out of limits! If you did get caught out by unforecast winds, any drift had to be counteracted by flying slightly wing down into the wind and touching down firmly on the into-wind mainwheel and tailwheel simultaneously; the other wheel dropped on at touchdown. I have landed with a 15kt crosswind without any problem, but 10kt

was always the maximum planned component. Tailwinds were avoided at all cost as they exacerbated any groundloop tendency.

d. Touch-and-go landings The potential disaster areas are too numerous to discuss. DON'T!

e. Rapid power increases during go-arounds Go-arounds were flown by smoothly increasing MAP to 1.1atm, selecting undercarriage UP with a positive rate of climb, selecting the prop to AUTO, then raising the flaps. If the throttle was increased too rapidly, full right aileron and almost full right rudder were required to maintain straight wings level flight. I suspect that it would have been possible to lose lateral and directional control if the throttle was opened too far and too quickly. It is definitely worth practising go-arounds when first converting to the aeroplane.

Summary

We only flew Black 6 from grass strips (except for one diversion due to excessive crosswind). The tailwheel was always locked for take-off and landing, and we did not plan to fly with crosswind components of more than 10kt, nor with tailwinds. I always tried to make smooth throttle inputs, and I had planned a strategy for radiator flap and propeller operations. Three-point landings were always attempted. Note that the Pilots' Notes or Pilots' Operating Handbook for other Bf109s or Buchóns may include advice that differs from the operating techniques which I have described. Obviously, the official document must be followed.

Comparing the Bf109E-4 with the Bf109G-2 (Trop): Flt Lt Charlie Brown

Charlie Brown is currently serving as an RAF pilot, and became involved in flying historic aircraft after being a Spitfire test/display pilot with Historic Flying Ltd at Audley End. He was then asked to become a display pilot for Black 6 and since then has gone on to fly other historic aircraft, including the Bf109E, and the Hawker Hurricane.

Aircraft systems

The aircraft systems are covered in great detail
elsewhere in this book so I shall only cover
them in so far as the salient differences between
the Bf109E and G models are concerned.

Cockpits

E model: lots of engine gauges and very basic
flight instruments (no artificial horizon and
no gyro compass). G model: fewer engine
gauges and excellent flight instruments (a very
advanced artificial horizon, which incorporates
a turn and slip indicator and a gyro compass
that is slaved to a magnetic detector unit); also
the cockpit of the G model is dominated by the
breech cover for the 20mm cannon which sits
between your legs.

Flaps

Plain flaps on both models, manually operated
by a wheel on the left-hand side of the cockpit.
In the E model, lowering the flaps also droops
the ailerons with the flaps up to 20°. In the G
model the ailerons do not droop with the flaps,
but both sets of radiator flaps do. Radiator flap
control: E model, manual by means of winding
handle on the right-hand side of the cockpit; G
model, hydraulic, by means of a selector on the
forward right-hand side of the cockpit. For the
G model there is a fully automatic setting for the
radiator flaps that opens and closes the flaps
in response to changes in the engine coolant
temperature.

Propeller control

Electrical for both models (the propeller pitch
indicator is a clock type gauge on the right-
hand side of the instrument panel . . . thus
propeller pitch settings are referred to as per
a clock, '12 o'clock' etc.). E model: one of
three modification states: 1. Manual control
by a switch in the centre of the instrument
panel; 2. Manual control by a rocker switch
on the throttle; 3. As per mod. State number
2, but with an automatic function by operating
a switch close to the throttle quadrant (in
automatic control an electrical governing system
matches propeller rpm settings to throttle
position). G model: as per mod. State 3.

Undercarriage

Hydraulic operation for both models. E model:
a rotary control on the right-hand side of the
instrument panel. G model: a pushbutton
control on the left-hand side of the instrument
panel. While on the subject of the Bf109
undercarriage, the Bf109 main undercarriage
design has a profound effect upon the aircraft's
handling, when taxiing, taking-off and landing.
The design allows for the wings to be removed
from the aircraft quickly and easily because
the main undercarriage is attached to the
fuselage at the engine bay firewall. This means
that the track of the mainwheels is narrow and
that the centre of gravity is well behind the
mainwheels, thus the aircraft are very tail heavy
and prone to be laterally unstable when on their
undercarriage.

Taxiing

The Bf109E and G both handle in a similar way
when taxiing. With so much weight bearing on
the tailwheel both aircraft are difficult to turn as
they would really rather continue in a straight
line. To put things into perspective, having just
moved off the chocks, the application of full
rudder and the corresponding wheel brake will
only lock the wheel brake, the aircraft will not
turn. To get the aircraft to turn you will need to
move the control column fully forward, use a
co-ordinated burst of power, rudder and brake
to get the tailwheel to castor and the aircraft to
turn (with the control column forward the burst
of power helps to relieve the weight on the
tailwheel. Directional control at normal taxiing

speeds is easier, but still the control column needs to be forward of neutral.

Taking-off

The take-off in any model of the Bf109 series of aircraft is not a manoeuvre to be taken lightly. The aircraft sit in a high nose attitude when on all three wheels (often referred to as being: 'on three points'). This means that if a take-off from three points were to be attempted the aircraft would be trying to get airborne in a semi-stalled condition. Thus at some point during the take-off roll the tail has to be raised so that the aircraft is in a slightly tail down attitude. At this point two things happen: first, the directional stabilising force provided by lots of weight bearing down on the tailwheel is lost the moment the tailwheel loses contact with the ground; second, there is a powerful gyroscopic precessional force caused by pitching the propeller disc which leads to yaw, that must be contained to maintain directional control.

The Bf109E is a much lighter aircraft than the G model and this is very apparent during the take-off. With the E model the tail is raised to the take-off attitude before the airspeed indicators' first marking, which is 60kmh (37mph), and the aircraft flies itself off the ground at 110kmh (68mph). In contrast with the G model the tail is best kept on the ground until 100kmh (62mph) and the aircraft can be flown off the ground at 150kmh (93mph).

As a slight aside, something that I remember being told in a light-hearted way, but that I subsequently found to be very true about the Bf109 series of aircraft is: 'If you survive the first take-off, you are likely to survive the landing.'

General handling

In pitch The elevator forces and stick force per 'g' for the E and the G models are very similar. The forces are relatively heavy, but by no means unusual when compared to other fighter aircraft of their time. Both models are fitted with auto slots which enable the wings to fly at a higher angle of attack than would otherwise be possible and help to prevent wing drop at the stall. The auto slots are fully automatic and cannot be locked by the pilot. It is the action of the auto slots that makes both aircraft relatively hard work and rather less than elegant to loop. The

elevator trimmer is powerful and effective and in both aircraft is operated by a wheel situated on the left-hand side of the cockpit, similar to and alongside, the flap operating wheel.

In yaw In yaw as in pitch, both aircraft feel and respond in a similar way. The rudder forces are not unduly heavy but there are quite large changes in directional trim (requiring the use of rudder to prevent yaw and keep the slip ball in the middle), with changes of power, airspeed and pitch (through precessional forces acting upon the propeller). Neither the E model nor the G-2 models have a rudder trim control in the cockpit.

In roll The E and G models have very different wing designs and it is when rolling the aircraft that this is most apparent in terms of the handling characteristics. The E model has light and very responsive ailerons and the rate of roll is quite remarkable; the G model's rate of roll is positively pedestrian in comparison.

Stalling Both aircraft are similarly relatively benign at the stall. Notwithstanding the operation of the auto slots, both aircraft give warning of the stall by providing airframe buffet, which is felt through the control column a small margin before the stall. Both aircraft show little tendency to drop a wing at the stall, though a small wing drop is likely in a stall in the approach configuration.

Approach and landing

The undercarriage and flap limiting speeds for both models is 250kmh (155mph). The downwind leg of the circuit is a busy time in a Bf109, as the flaps have to be lowered manually against the airflow (which takes several turns of the flap wheel). The final approach is best flown as a continuous gentle turn to aid the pilot's visibility.

The speeds to fly on the final approach are very different:

E model Start the final turn at 160kmh (99mph), halfway around aim for 140kmh (87mph) and a threshold speed of 120kmh (75mph).

G model Start the final turn at 200kmh (124mph), halfway around at 180kmh (112mph) and a threshold speed of 160kmh (99mph).

The large difference in the approach speeds is a function of weight, wing design and the drooping ailerons of the E model.

Summary

My first experience of the Bf109 series of aircraft was with Black 6, a G-2 model which I had the privilege to fly for a number of years before I had the unique opportunity of conducting all the post restoration flight testing of the then one-and-only airworthy E model (an E-4) in the world. The comments above are based upon my first-hand experience of both aircraft. I have to say that I was surprised just how different the two aircraft proved to be.

Luftwaffe Bf109 pilot: Eduard Isken

Eduard Isken was a pilot in the Luftwaffe fighter wing JG77 which Black 6 was attached to. His reminiscence of the period during which Black 6 was captured by British forces is an interesting testimonial to the latter stages of the war in North Africa for a German Bf109 fighter pilot. This period was characterised, on the German side, by almost constant retreat and the developing fight against increasingly vastly superior numbers of Allied aircraft. In the main, the German pilots were happy with their Bf109s, which were the best Axis fighters available to them in numbers at that stage of the war in North Africa. Nevertheless, against increasingly overwhelming numbers of Allied fighters of growing quality and firepower, and faced with shortages of equipment due to the logistical difficulties of obtaining supplies from the Italian mainland, the German fighter pilots in North Africa were up against increasingly hopeless odds.

In October and November 1942 the 3rd Gruppe of fighter wing JG77 (III/JG77) was stationed in the area of El Daba at several air strips. The missions flown at that time were in support of the Africa Corps at El Alamein. In November the positions of the German-Italian forces were overrun and the big offensive of the Allied ground forces started, as well as offensive operations by the RAF. For us the time of a fighting retreat had commenced. When and where Black 6 was left behind by us, I cannot tell. My guess is El Kasaba, Bir-el-Acra

or Gambut. From these places missions were flown against fighter and bomber planes of the RAF as well as [Allied] ground forces. While located at these airfields we also endured continuous strong attacks by the RAF with fighter-bombers, Spitfires and Kittyhawks [American-built Curtiss P-40 Warhawks operated by the British as Kittyhawks]. Without doubt the Black 6 from our 8th Squadron (8./JG77), flown by Leutnant Ludemann, must not have been operable and had to be left behind.

At the end of February 1943 our III/JG77 was stationed at the airport of Matmata south of Gabès in Tunisia. During the first month of 1943 the Americans from the west started their first air raids on German positions and supply routes. As a result we had to try and survive bombardments by the RAF as well as the Americans. At that time our aircraft escorted Junkers Ju87 'Stukas' attacking American positions at Faid. Thereafter the Americans increased their air attacks on our airfields with Boeing Fortresses. Our pilots at this time had some successes in combat against the Boeing Fortresses, Lightnings, Marauders, Spitfires and Hurricanes. During the first days of March the air activities of the RAF increased again, and English tank forces advanced from the east out of the area of Tripoli. Our planes were involved in the defensive action against enemy bomber and fighter forces, as well as flying protective cover for our own Luftwaffe forces.

In the middle of March our main task was the support for our own infantry and armoured forces in the area of Medenine. On 10 March 1943 our 10th Squadron (10./JG77) was operating in the area of Medenine with the aid of hunting and raiding [an equivalent of the seek and destroy tactics used by the Allies]. Leutnant Ludemann did not return. According to the combat reports there were dog-fights with American Lightnings. Against the joint force of American and RAF aircraft which were by now far superior in number to our own, a heroic battle was fought until the end in Tunisia.

Author's note: Isken concludes his narrative by saying, 'I want to point out that in the fights with RAF pilots there was always fairness, which was very much respected on our part.'

Flying the Bf109G: Capt Eric 'Winkle' Brown RN

One of Britain's most celebrated test pilots, Captain Eric 'Winkle' Brown CBE, DSC, AFC, MA, RN, flew many types of Allied aircraft, in addition to a range of captured Axis aircraft, during the Second World War and immediately after. He shared his thoughts on the Bf109 in conversation with co-author Malcolm V. Lowe in 2003.

O ne of the Bf109s that Eric Brown flew was a Bf109G-6/U2 Werk Nummer 412951, which was captured during 1944 and was allocated the British military serial number TP814. Although he felt that the Bf109 as a fighting machine looked purposeful and even lethal, its small size was an important consideration with its cramped cockpit which he referred to often as being 'claustrophobic', with limited room to move even for a pilot of comparatively small stature such as Eric Brown himself. Nevertheless the aircraft functioned effectively, despite the somewhat primitive means of starting the engine. All Bf109s had a manual start-up in which a ground crew member had to crank a removable handle which, in the case of the Bf109G-6, engaged a flywheel inertia starting system located on the right-hand side of the engine. Employing 1.3ata (atmospheres or pressure in kg per square cm) of boost and 15 degrees of flap, the take-off run was relatively short and was better than the Spitfire Mk.IX that he was particularly familiar with at that time. The Bf109 always performed best on a grass surface, but the type's marked swing to the left on take-off had to be watched continually and counteracted with rudder movement, and over the years was the source of many pilots, both novice and experienced, being caught out. In any case, the Messerschmitt could not be left to its own devices while on its take-off run and needed to be flown off smoothly rather than being aggressively pulled off into the air. After that the hydraulically activated undercarriage was retracted the Bf109 would climb away effectively, as it was a good performer in the air once the tricky part – taking off – had been accomplished. Then there was always the landing to think about a little later.

BELOW: **The instrument panel and gun sight of a Bf109E (probably a Bf109E-4) showing the compact nature of the instrumentation – there was little room for anything more complicated or bulky. The central panel below the instrument panel was associated with bomb-aiming, suggesting that this is the cockpit of a fighter-bomber Bf109E-4 or E-7.** *Malcolm V. Lowe Collection*

As a fighting machine Eric Brown found the Bf109G to be 'a delight to fly, but diving was a weakness, with the controls becoming very heavy as speed built up'. He also found that the wing leading edge slats, which were actually based on a Handley Page Patent for leading edge 'slots', were sometimes more of a hindrance than a help. These operated automatically and theoretically gave more control during low-speed flight and manoeuvres, but they would sometimes operate asymmetrically, particularly if the aircraft was pulled early into the air on its take-off run, or during air combat manoeuvring if too much elevator was used. In fact, he found the harmony of the various flight controls to be poor, with the elevators being heavy, the rudder too light, and the ailerons being light and prone to 'snatching' (moving unexpectedly quickly or harshly) if the wing leading edge slats opened

asymmetrically in combat manoeuvres. This latter point in particular made the Bf109 not a very good gun platform, particularly during dog-fighting, although it was well-mannered and stable in level flight at virtually all levels. The slats could also come open on occasion if the Bf109 was flown in the slipstream of another aircraft, which was not a very good trait for a fighter which was supposed to come up behind its quarry.

The stall was comparatively gentle, and occurred at altitude at approximately 105mph (169kmh) with the engine throttled back and with the fuel tanks half-empty. When the stall was neared there would be very noticeable elevator buffeting and the opening of the slats, which would sometimes open asymmetrically and make the stall more difficult to control due to the resulting aileron 'snatching'. On landing, the stall speed was 99mph (159kmh). The landing itself was a much less happy experience.

Countless pilots have found the act of landing the Bf109 to be something of a nightmare, and Eric Brown, with all his experience and airmanship skills, was none too impressed either. Care in particular was needed on the approach as forward view over the nose was poor and the aircraft would readily balloon up off the surface if it hit uneven ground on touchdown, there being a surplus of lift even with the rather more extensive wing-flaps arrangement of the Bf109F and G-series. Nevertheless, landings needed to be made on grass wherever possible, preferably without a crosswind, but the aircraft would happily head off in its own direction with its narrow-track undercarriage and tendency for an undercarriage leg to buckle if touched down too hard on one side.

Overall, Eric Brown felt that the Bf109G probably represented the Bf109 series after it had reached its best, but that it could still be a formidable opponent if flown well. Nevertheless, it did not warrant inclusion in his list of the top three fighters of the Second World War that he had flown – which were the Supermarine Spitfire (particularly in its later models), the Focke-Wulf Fw190 in its late-war Fw190D-9 development, and the North American P-51 Mustang.

Start-up and shut-down

Start-up procedure
Ground running and start-up for flying follow the same procedure except where stated.

1 Park the aircraft into wind, making sure the area is clear in front and behind.
2 Make sure the aircraft is chocked and that all intakes and bungs are removed.
3 Position fire extinguisher and ground power set if required.
4 Tie down the tail (ground running only).
5 Pull the prop through five blades by hand; this must only be carried out with a cold engine and after checking that the mag switch is OFF.
6 Pilot does a walk round check, making sure that all panels are secured, and that all flying controls move freely.

Cockpit checks
1 Canopy is closed and locked.
2 Trim is fully nose up.
3 Flaps are up.
4 Throttle is closed.
5 Tailwheel lock is engaged.
6 The fuel cocks (P1, P2) are closed.
7 The prop pitch is set to manual.
8 The magneto M1+M2 check OFF (0).
9 Undercarriage selector is in the neutral position, both buttons gated.
10 Radiator control set to AUTO.
11 Electrics circuit breaker panel is OFF and all circuit breakers in the OUT position.
12 Power ON.

13 Circuit breakers set to ON as required.
14 Check fuel and temperature gauges are reading.
15 Radio set to ON.

16 Check undercarriage indicator for two green lights.
17 Prop pitch set to 1230 (fully fine).

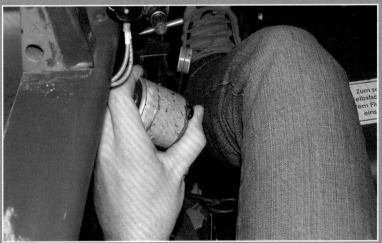

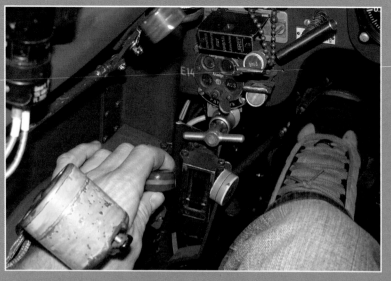

18 Fuel cocks set to P1, P2.

19 Ground crew member will start winding
the starter handle, located on the
starboard side of the engine.
20 Move the throttle to one third open and
lock with the friction damper.

21 Fuel pump switch ON, watch pressure
rise to 0.3kg/cm^2.

22 Prime the engine when the starter is fully
wound, with approximately six full strokes
of the priming pump.
23 Call 'Clear prop', the ground crew on the
wing will remove the starting handle and
jump off the rear of the wing.
24 Set the magneto switch to M1, M2 and
pull the starter switch.

25 When the engine fires, release the starter and adjust the throttle to 600rpm.

26 Make sure that the oil pressure rises within ten seconds and is below 8kgcm^2.
27 Warm up the engine, check the operation of radiator cooler flaps and check instruments for readings.
28 Readings should be: fuel pressure=1.5–1.8kg/cm^2; oil pressure=3.5–8kg/cm^2; oil temperature=75°C; coolant temperature=60–105°C.

Engine performance prior to take-off

To test engine performance before take-off, the propeller must be coarsened to the 12 o'clock position and a mag drop check is carried out at 1,900rpm. The rpm gauge should not drop more than 50rpm.

Shut-down checks

1 Pull the plug cleaner for five seconds at 1,800rpm
2 Run the engine for two minutes at 1,000rpm, do not shut down with a temperature of 115°C or above.

3 Operate the idle cut-out until the propeller stops, then reset.
4 Set the magneto switch to OFF (0).
5 Shut the fuel cock to OFF.
6 Trip the circuit breakers and switch power off.
7 Engage the control locks.

Gefüllt mit Fl.-D.

1918

Vorsicht beim Öffnen
Kühler ist im Haubenteil eingebaut

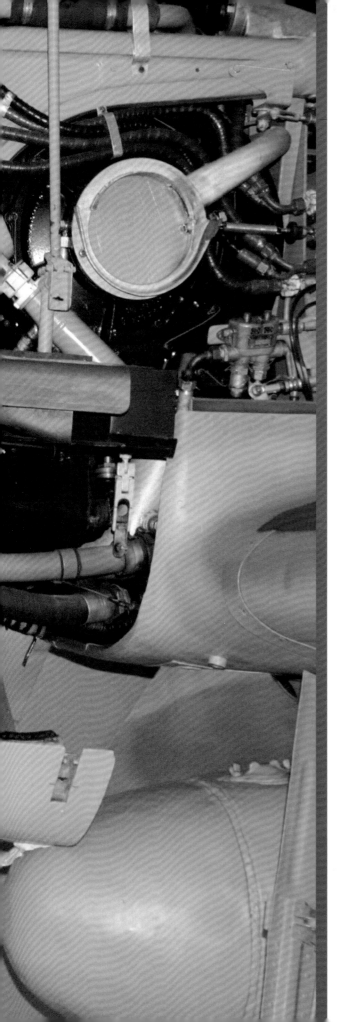

Chapter Six

The engineer's view

Paul Blackah was one of the team of skilled volunteers who worked on Black 6 and successfully returned this historic aircraft to airworthy condition. He currently works on the RAF Battle of Britain Memorial Flight and is co-author of this book.

When Black 6 arrived at Benson in 1983 and was allocated hangar space next to the structures bay where Paul was working, he didn't realise that it would spark a passion that would still be with him over 25 years later and lead to his current job on the Battle of Britain Memorial Flight.

LEFT: The engine cowlings are easy to open, giving good access to the engine and its components. *Matthew Starr*

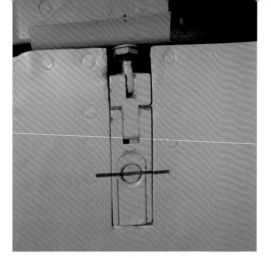

From my perspective: Paul Blackah

I first started by taking structural items to strip down and rebuild, such as radiator fairings and engine cowlings, then it progressed to being involved in the installation of systems and eventually becoming a full-time volunteer member of the team; working many weekends until eventually Black 6 was airworthy and cleared to display at air shows. My role then changed to supporting her at the many air shows that she attended and carrying out routine maintenance.

I'm often asked about the major differences between the Bf109G-2 and the Spitfire/Hurricane from an engineer's perspective. Each aircraft has its good and bad points; the biggest difference is that the Messerschmitt's main components are more easily accessible. The engine compartment can be accessed by undoing eight quick release fasteners, the lower cowling then swings down and exposes the oil cooler and the underside of the engine. The two side cowlings hinge upwards and are held in place with a bonnet stay. All this takes less than a minute to accomplish. With some marks of Spitfire, you could still be there, decowling the engine, anything from 15 to 30 minutes later.

Other parts of the aircraft can also be accessed for inspection as easily as this, as there are a number of panels with quick release latches.

All the electrical components on the 109 are wired up with plugs and sockets, making disconnection fast and efficient compared to having to find a terminal block and undoing the individual wires to remove the item on a Spitfire/Hurricane.

The fluid and gas systems are colour coded, for instance fuel is yellow, oil is red/brown, coolant is green, which makes pipework easy to identify on the 109.

The cockpit layout for the 109 pilot is laid out in a more logical way than the Spitfire and the Hurricane and some of the systems, such as the oil cooler control and radiator control, are automatic to reduce stress on the pilot. It is of note that the 109 has a cockpit floor, unlike the Spitfire and Hurricane, which have two running boards for the pilot's feet.

On the other hand, a Spitfire or Hurricane canopy does not weigh as much as the 109's, and allows better visibility for the pilot, and they are easier to open and close. The seat is also adjustable by the pilot, whereas the 109's seat has three positions, which have to be set before flight and cannot be readjusted while in flight.

The Merlin appears to be a more reliable engine than the Daimler-Benz; the Merlin servicing cycle is 500 hours between overhauls, compared to the Daimler-Benz, which is 200 hours. The Daimler-Benz engine has to have the block rings retightened every 12½ hours, which means the engine on a 109 needs more attention.

If I had to make a choice between the Spitfire, Hurricane and the Bf109G-2, then I would probably choose the 109, simply for ease of access from an engineer's view, however I enjoy working on all the aircraft despite, or perhaps regardless of, their individual quirks and foibles.'

Airframe

The 109 is a low wing monoplane of all metal construction, with two hydraulically operated undercarriage legs retracting outwards into the wings. For the purpose of this book, we will examine each major section of the aircraft individually.

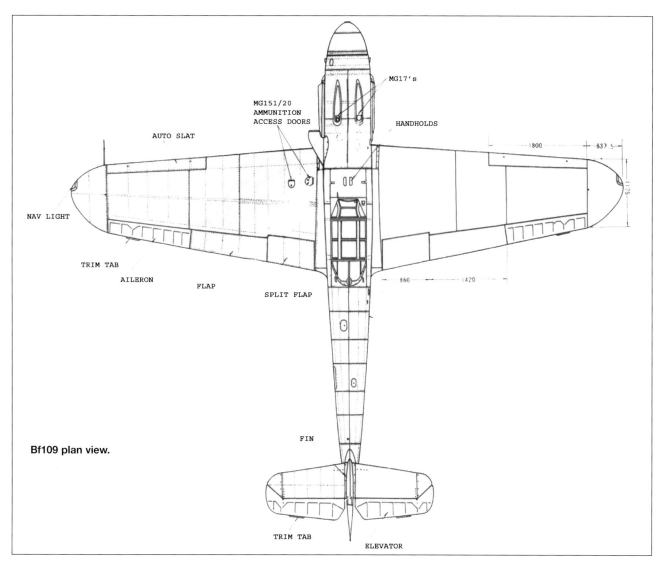

MG151/20
AMMUNITION
ACCESS DOORS

MG17's

HANDHOLDS

AUTO SLAT

NAV LIGHT

TRIM TAB

AILERON

FLAP

SPLIT FLAP

1800
637.5
1175

860
1420

FIN

Bf109 plan view.

TRIM TAB

ELEVATOR

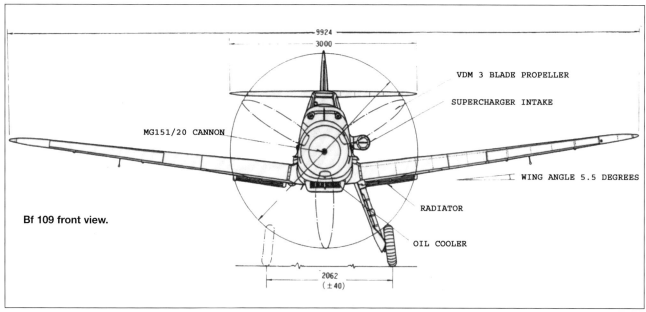

9924
3000

VDM 3 BLADE PROPELLER

SUPERCHARGER INTAKE

MG151/20 CANNON

WING ANGLE 5.5 DEGREES

RADIATOR

Bf 109 front view.

OIL COOLER

2062
(±40)

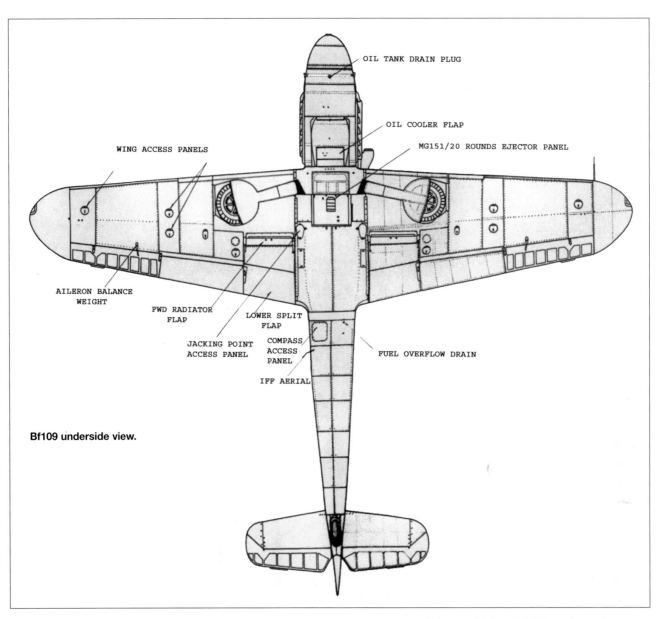

OIL TANK DRAIN PLUG

OIL COOLER FLAP

MG151/20 ROUNDS EJECTOR PANEL

WING ACCESS PANELS

AILERON BALANCE
WEIGHT

FWD RADIATOR
FLAP

LOWER SPLIT
FLAP

JACKING POINT
ACCESS PANEL

COMPASS
ACCESS
PANEL

FUEL OVERFLOW DRAIN

IFF AERIAL

Bf109 underside view.

RIGHT: Starboard side of the fuselage. The hole in the forward bulkhead is for the MG151 20mm cannon breach. *Black 6 Team*

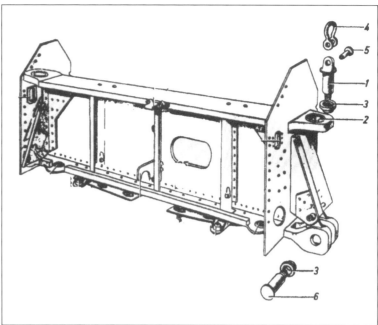

ABOVE LEFT: Front bulkhead casting and structure. *Black 6 Team*

ABOVE: Spar centre section. *Ersatzteil-Liste Bf109G-2*

LEFT: The stripped back fuselage. *Black 6 Team*

Fuselage

The fuselage consists of forward and rear sections, which are riveted together to form a complete unit.

The forward section (cockpit) is of a general flat-sided duralumin skin, 1.2mm (18swg), construction, which is put together using countersunk 120° rivets and supports the jettisonable canopy assembly and windscreen. Attached, at the front of this section, is the main engine bulkhead. On this bulkhead is a support frame for the gun mountings for the MG17 machine guns and ammunition boxes.

To the middle of the main engine bulkhead, lower edge, is mounted the spar bearer with

LEFT: Fuselage engine bulkhead. *Black 6 Team*

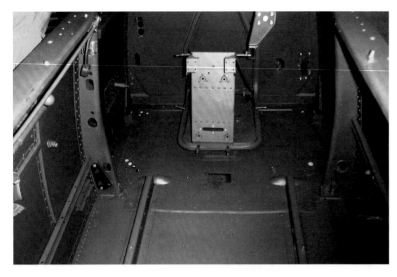

ABOVE: The cockpit floor of a Buchón with stripped-out interior. *Airframe Assemblies*

RIGHT: Co-author Paul working in the fuel tank bay. Note the two armour plates bolted behind the pilot's seat. *Black 6 Team*

FAR RIGHT: Inside the rear fuselage looking aft from the fuel tank bay. The three clips at the top are for the oxygen bottles. *Black 6 Team*

RIGHT: Fuselage lower foot step. *Matthew Starr*

FAR RIGHT: Fuselage upper hand hold. *Matthew Starr*

RIGHT: Fuselage step panel in the open position. The canvas zipped cover allows the engineer to inspect areas inside the fuselage. *Matthew Starr*

FAR RIGHT: Starting handle in place. *Matthew Starr*

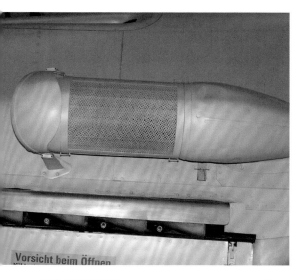

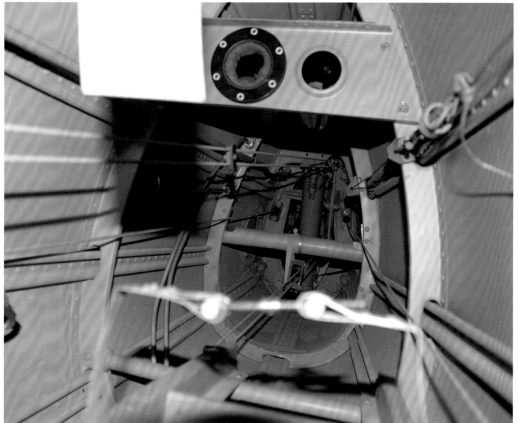

Hier
anheben →

~ WE

Hier
aufbocken

Reifendruck 4,5 atü

8

9

ABOVE LEFT: Tropical filter attached to the supercharger intake to stop debris entering the supercharger on take-off, landing and when taxying.
Matthew Starr

ABOVE: Rear fuselage lifting point. The black band underneath is the trestle marking.
Matthew Starr

LEFT: Rear fuselage looking aft. The top of the picture shows the rear rifle mount and further down, the tail leg. The tie rods are the elevator and rudder controls.
Matthew Starr

two tubular struts. This area also served to mount the main undercarriage leg supports. On the underside of the bulkhead there is also a fitting for the attachment of the bearers for the drop tank and the securing of the bomb installation.

The lower portion of the forward section of the fuselage comprises cockpit floor, wing and fuselage fillet fairings. Beneath the cockpit floor runs the spar centre section, which is connected to the fuselage side walls with riveted brackets. Also housed in this section is the fuel tank and a luggage compartment.

The rear fuselage is of monocoque construction, 1mm (19-gauge), consisting of two halves that are preformed and joined together with top and bottom longerons. The construction, as a whole, is flush-riveted

together using 120° rivets. On the left-hand side there is a hatch through which the radio equipment, oxygen bottles and compressed air bottles are accessible.

Tail section

This section consists of the tailplane carrier, the fin and the tailplane. Bolted to the rear fuselage frame is the tailplane carrier, and the fin is then secured on to it using bolts, as is the pivoting tailplane. The carrier also serves as the installation point for fitting a retractable tail leg.

The fin is constructed from two dural sheet halves with a hinge section riveted on each half, and joined with a hinge pin. In order to counteract the airscrew torque, the profile is designed to be asymmetric

Mainplanes

The mainplane is of all metal construction, consisting of solid main and auxiliary spars, to which the ribs are riveted. The skin, which is dural sheet, is then riveted to the main, auxiliary spars and the ribs using the flush riveting technique. The wing to fuselage fittings are made of steel and are riveted to the upper and lower spar flanges.

Incorporated into each wing is a strut channel and a wheel recess, which allows the landing gear to be retracted into the wing during flight.

ABOVE:
Re-skinned tail unit.
Airframe Assemblies

RIGHT: The area around the wheel bay with top skin removed.
Airframe Assemblies

RIGHT: Starboard wing inboard rib. *Black 6 Team*

BELOW: Upper spar with wing attachment bracket pinned to jig. The space above the spar is for the radiator and fairing assembly. *Airframe Assemblies*

ABOVE: Wing underside inboard with skins removed. *Airframe Assemblies*

LEFT: Inboard wing trailing edge with coolant radiator fairing removed. *Black 6 Team*

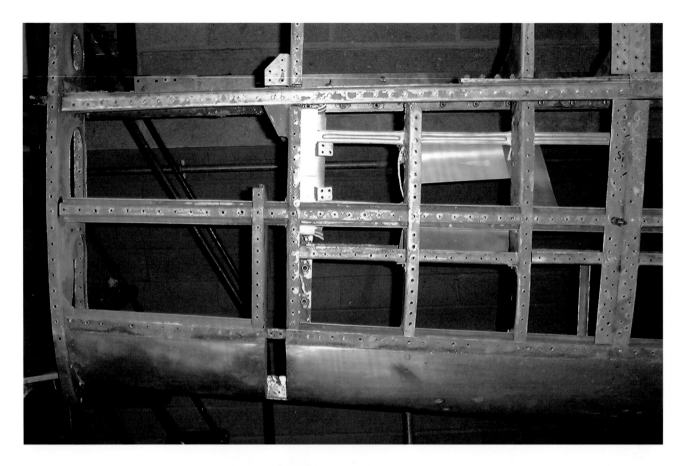

ABOVE: Leading edge structure. The slot is for the outboard slat roller assembly. *Airframe Assemblies*

On the trailing edge of the wings, the ailerons are attached between ribs nine and thirteen. The landing flaps are located between ribs four and eight. Between the fuselage and the landing flaps, the cooler gills operate on the lower sides of the wing trailing edges.

Leading edge slats are mounted on the leading edge in the region of ribs eight to thirteen. Detachable wing tips, in which the navigation lights are mounted, complete the structure of the wings. The port wing tip also houses the Pitot head. All systems built into the wing are accessible through lockable access panels on the underside of the wings.

RIGHT: Quick-release inspection access panel. The two holes are for picketing the aircraft in strong winds. *Matthew Starr*

FAR RIGHT: Lower wing attachment. The small cup to the left is the jacking point. *Matthew Starr*

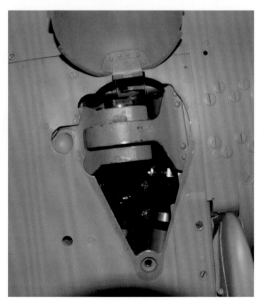

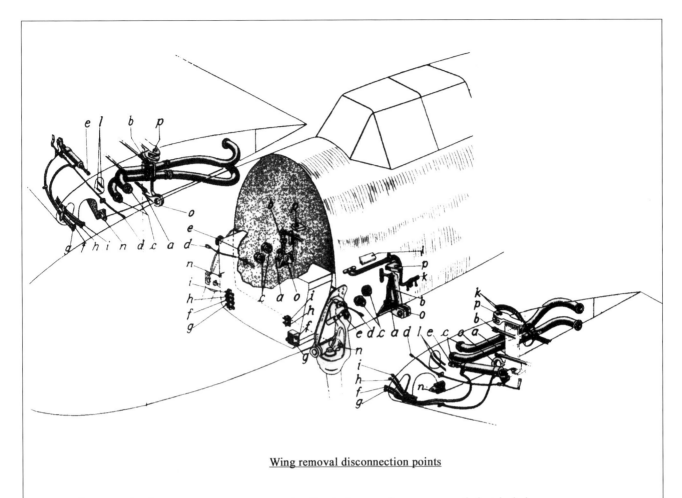

Wing removal disconnection points

a flap control rods
b aileron control rods
c coolant pipes
d u/c emergency release cables

e retraction jack eye ends
f/g retraction jack hyd pipes
h/i flap jack hyd pipes
k pitot static pipes

l electrical plugs
n forward wing attachment bolts
o lower wing attachment bolts
p upper wing attachment bolts

ABOVE: Wing removal disconnection points.
D(Luft)T.2109 G-2

LEFT: Wing leading edge slat in the open position, looking up.
Matthew Starr

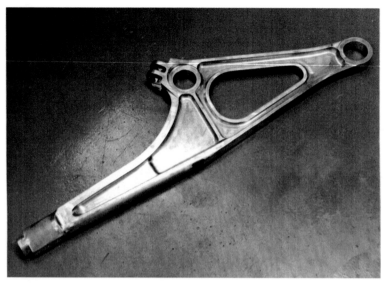

Engine bearer

The engine bearer consists of two cast Elektron alloy beams and three tubular struts. These beams are attached, using rubber mounts, to the side of the engine and the rear of each beam is attached to the top of the fuselage engine bulkhead.

Two of the tubular struts attach to the engine beams and to the fuselage. The third acts as a bracing strut to the starboard one.

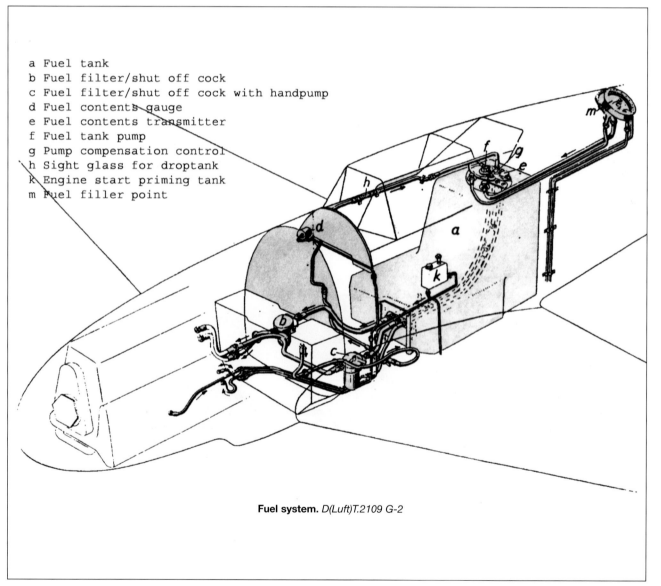

a Fuel tank
b Fuel filter/shut off cock
c Fuel filter/shut off cock with handpump
d Fuel contents gauge
e Fuel contents transmitter
f Fuel tank pump
g Pump compensation control
h Sight glass for droptank
k Engine start priming tank
m Fuel filler point

Fuel system. *D(Luft)T.2109 G-2*

Fuel

The fuel is held in a 400-litre rubber self-sealing fuel tank, which is fitted under and behind the pilot's seat. The filling point for this tank is situated at the top left of the rear fuselage, between frames two and three. A fuel pump and a fuel quantity gauge transmitter is fitted into the tank.

The fuel ON/OFF lever is situated on the left-hand side of the cockpit in the throttle box. This lever operates two fuel cocks/filters, which can either be selected individually or used together. There is a low-level fuel warning light on the instrument panel, which lights up when the quantity of fuel is less than 100 litres, to warn

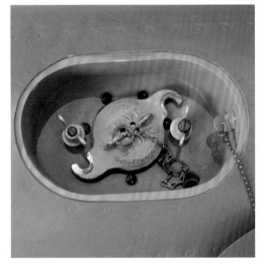

ABOVE LEFT: New (left) and original fuel tanks. *Black 6 Team*

ABOVE: Fuel tank bay. *Black 6 Team*

LEFT: Fuel filling point on the rear fuselage. *Matthew Starr*

LEFT: The aircraft is raised at the tail, ready to calibrate the fuel tank contents. *Black 6 Team*

BELOW: **Coolant system.** *D(Luft)T.2109 G-2*

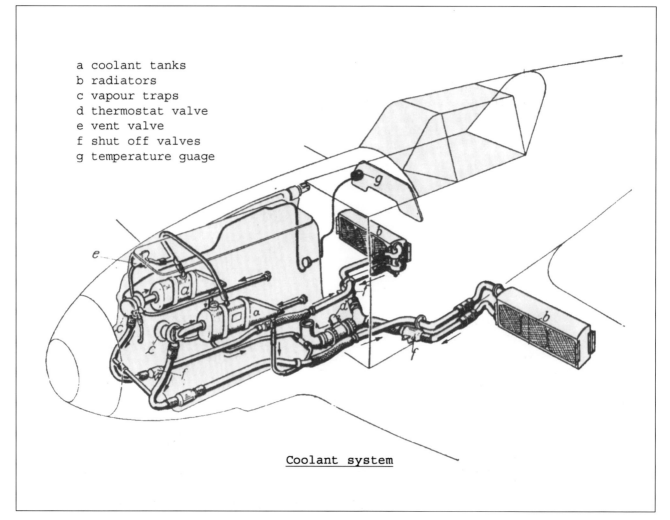

a coolant tanks
b radiators
c vapour traps
d thermostat valve
e vent valve
f shut off valves
g temperature guage

Coolant system

LEFT: **Coolant tank filler cap.** *Matthew Starr*

the pilot that he has approximately 20 minutes of flying time remaining.

A drop tank can be fitted to allow an extra 300 litres of fuel to be carried. This is controlled by a lever, mounted on the left-hand wall of the cockpit, and a valve, mounted forward of the cockpit front wall.

Coolant

The coolant system comprises two coolant tanks, one on each side of the engine. The two tanks are connected by an expansion line. Each tank has a vapour trap mounted on the delivery line to the engine. On each of the lower surfaces of the port and starboard wings is a radiator and behind each of these is a cooler flap, which is mounted above and below in the wing.

To the front of the radiator is another cooler flap. All the flaps are operated by a hydraulic actuator, which is controlled by a thermostat in the coolant delivery line and operated by the pilot, using a rotary control within the cockpit on the lower right-hand side. The pilot can open and close the flaps or he can leave them in automatic where they will operate themselves. For example, if the aircraft was turned into a dive, the pilot would manually close the flaps to reduce drag. The rear cooler flaps are linked to the landing flaps, so that on lowering the landing flaps, the cooler flaps are also lowered.

The coolant temperature is registered by a thermocouple fitted in the starboard vapour trap and a temperature gauge fitted on the right-hand side of the instrument panel.

If one of the radiators fails due to leakage, the flow of coolant to and from the radiator concerned can be shut off to prevent the loss of the system coolant. Four coolant shut-off valves are fitted into the delivery and return lines, and are operated by two handles in the cockpit.

BELOW: **Starboard coolant radiator with forward and rear flaps.** *Matthew Starr*

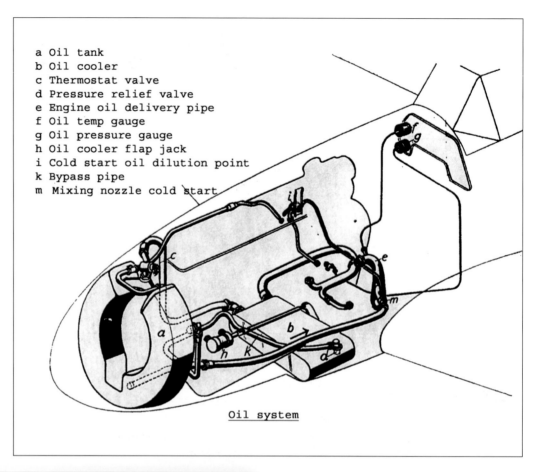

RIGHT: Oil system.

D(Luft)T.2109 G-2

a Oil tank
b Oil cooler
c Thermostat valve
d Pressure relief valve
e Engine oil delivery pipe
f Oil temp gauge
g Oil pressure gauge
h Oil cooler flap jack
i Cold start oil dilution point
k Bypass pipe
m Mixing nozzle cold start

Oil system

BELOW: Main oil feed pipe from the oil tank.

Matthew Starr

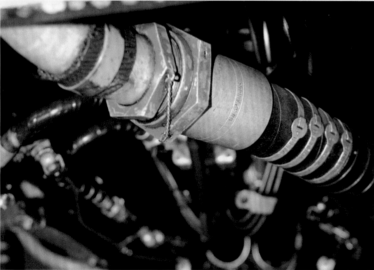

Main fluids and pressures

Fuel	100 Octane low lead avgas
Coolant	50% glycol/AL3 and 50% distilled water
Hydraulic oil	OM15
Engine oil	Aeroshell oil, semi-synthetic W15W-50

Oil

The oil system is a forced oil circulating system, driven by a gear pump located on the engine. A filter for removing debris is located to the rear of the pump. The oil tank itself is located at the front of the engine and holds 36 litres.

An oil cooler is fitted in the lower engine cowling. The oil temperature is controlled by a cooler flap, located on the lower engine cowling, operated by a hydraulic jack, which are controlled automatically by a thermostat fitted to the top of the oil tank.

To prevent the oil system from over pressurising, a relief valve and bypass line are fitted to the cooler. At a given pressure the oil is redirected back to the tank. The oil temperature is taken from a thermocouple incorporated within the oil delivery pipe, and recorded on a gauge to the right of the instrument panel.

The oil pressure line leads from the oil pump on the engine directly to a gauge on the right-hand side of the instrument panel.

Vorsicht beim Öffnen
Kühler ist im Haubenteil eingebaut

ABOVE LEFT: A warning that care should be taken when opening the lower engine cowl because the heavy oil cooler is fitted inside. *Matthew Starr*

ABOVE: Oil cooler flap operating jack. This jack operates automatically when the oil becomes hot, opening the flap, and then closing it again when the oil cools. *Matthew Starr*

LEFT: Oil filler cap and dipstick. The manufacturer's label is clearly shown. *Matthew Starr*

BELOW: Engine oil tank. The red valve at the top is the thermostat for the oil cooler flap. *Matthew Starr*

LEFT: Oil tank filling point. *Matthew Starr*

BELOW: Oil cooler flap thermostat valve. *Matthew Starr*

ABOVE: Propeller hub and spinner back plate. Note the cannon blast tube and the propeller pitch gear wheel mechanism.
Black 6 Team

RIGHT: Inside the spinner with blast tube support diaphragm.
Matthew Starr

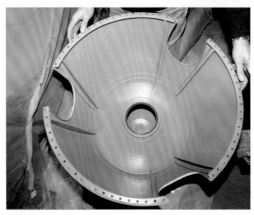

FAR RIGHT: Propeller spinner. Note the 20mm cannon flash tube at the front.
Matthew Starr

Propeller

The propeller is a metal three-bladed variable pitch airscrew, manufactured by VDM. The type specified for the Bf109G-2 was the VDM 9-12087 A. Control of the pitch setting is operated by an electrical motor, which is operated by the pilot using a switch attached to the throttle. The propeller hub is covered with a spinner, which attaches to a base plate fitted to the back of the hub.

Electrics

The electrical system is a 24-volt system and is powered by a battery, fitted in a tray

RIGHT: Electrical circuit breaker panel. Each one operates an individual system.
Matthew Starr

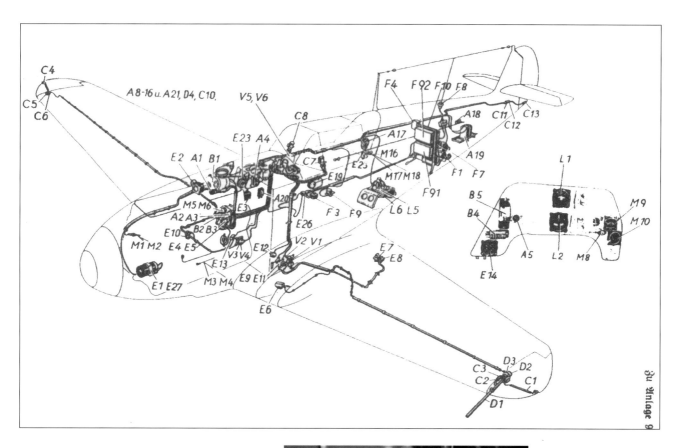

A 8-16 u. A 21, D 4, C 10.

within the rear fuselage, and a generator mounted on the accessory drive of the engine. A circuit breaker panel is fitted to the right-hand side of the cockpit wall and each circuit breaker operates an individual system within the aircraft. A further remote controlled circuit breaker, situated in the rear

ABOVE:

Electrical system.
D(Luft)T.2109 G-2

FAR LEFT: Main power on/off circuit breaker located in the rear fuselage.
Matthew Starr

LEFT: The letters and numbers indicate the different electrical systems on the engine.
Matthew Starr

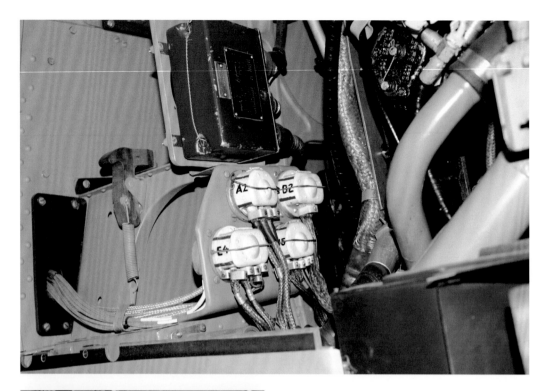

RIGHT: Engine system electrical plugs. They are painted white with red lines to indicate items that require disconnection prior to engine removal. *Matthew Starr*

RIGHT: Looking forward in the rear fuselage at the FuG7 radio. *Matthew Starr*

fuselage, isolates the battery from the aircraft circuits.

The following systems are operated electrically: the prop pitch mechanism, the armament system, fuel tank pump, cockpit lighting, engine monitoring systems, flight monitoring systems and navigation instruments and equipment. All instruments and main brake points are fitted with plugs and sockets for ease of fitment and removal.

Hydraulics

This system operates the undercarriage, the inboard radiator split flaps, and the oil cooler flap and is powered by a hydraulic pump fitted to the rear of the engine. The hydraulic oil tank is situated on the port side of the engine and the undercarriage selector valve is fitted on the forward face of the engine bulkhead, and is

RIGHT: Oil cooler flap jack in the lower cowling. *Matthew Starr*

FAR RIGHT: Hydraulic reservoir mounted onto the left-hand engine bearer. *Matthew Starr*

LEFT: Undercarriage selector valve hydraulic pressure relief valve and pipework.
Matthew Starr

BELOW:

Hydraulic system.
D(Luft)T.2109 G-2

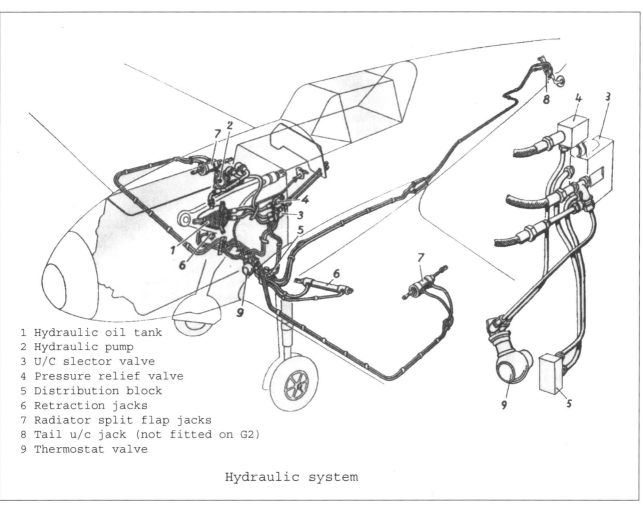

1 Hydraulic oil tank
2 Hydraulic pump
3 U/C selector valve
4 Pressure relief valve
5 Distribution block
6 Retraction jacks
7 Radiator split flap jacks
8 Tail u/c jack (not fitted on G2)
9 Thermostat valve

Hydraulic system

UNDERCARRIAGE LEG ASSEMBLY

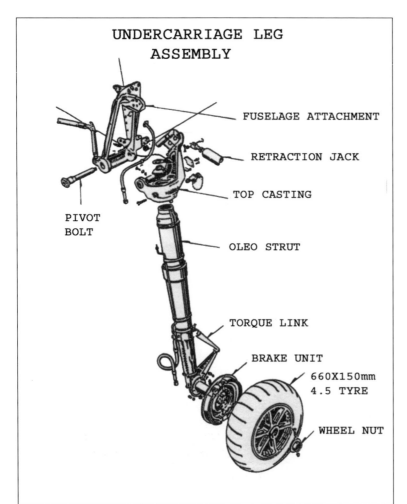

FUSELAGE ATTACHMENT

RETRACTION JACK

TOP CASTING

PIVOT BOLT

OLEO STRUT

TORQUE LINK

BRAKE UNIT

660X150mm 4.5 TYRE

WHEEL NUT

controlled by two push buttons on the left-hand side of the cockpit. By pushing in one of the buttons, the undercarriage is raised. Pressure builds up and pushes the button back out, which indicates to the pilot that the legs are raised. The same applies when the legs are lowered. A lever located on the right-hand side of the cockpit operates radiator flaps.

Quick release fittings between the selector valve and the hydraulic tank allow the fitment of a ground test rig.

Undercarriage

Two cantilever oleo struts, which are air- and oil-filled, are attached to mounting brackets, which are bolted to the forward fuselage bulkhead and side walls. Two door fairings are fitted to both legs and attached to these legs are retraction

LEFT: Starboard undercarriage mounting attachment.
Black 6 Team

RIGHT TOP: Cast alloy main wheel fitted with the original Continental tyre.
Jim Douthwaite

RIGHT: Undercarriage leg complete with original Continental tyre. Note the hydraulic brake pipe coming down the front of the leg.
Matthew Starr

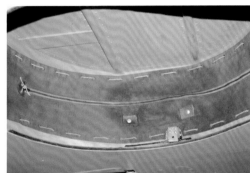

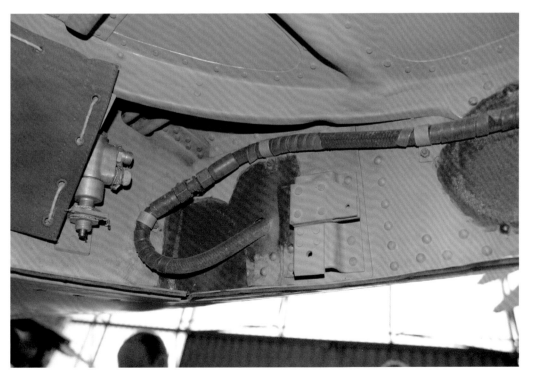

TOP LEFT: Leather protected flexible brake hose. *Matthew Starr*

TOP RIGHT: Starboard undercarriage up-lock and micro switch. *Matthew Starr*

CENTRE LEFT: Undercarraige bay showing the top of the undercarriage leg. The gold-coloured item in the hole is the retraction jack. *Matthew Starr*

CENTRE RIGHT: Wheel bay canvas shroud with zipped access to the hydraulic hoses. *Matthew Starr*

LEFT: Inside the undercarriage bay. The pipe work and the disconnected valve are for outer doors not fitted on the Bf109G-2. *Matthew Starr*

ABOVE: Wheel bay: warning – only fit tyres of this size.
Matthew Starr

ABOVE RIGHT: Tail-leg complete with cable-operated locking mechanism.
Matthew Starr

OPPOSITE PAGE: Undercarriage leg complete with door and brake unit.
Black 6 Team

jacks mounted in the wings. This installation allows the removal of the wings, leaving the undercarriage attached to support the fuselage for ease of transport.

When the undercarriage is retracted it is held in the wing by the uplock (located on the leg), which engages with a catch within the undercarriage bay. In the event of the failure of the hydraulic system, an emergency handle located on the left-hand side of the cockpit can release the undercarriage. This cable-operated system releases the catches in the wing and

allows the undercarriage to lower under its own weight into the fully down position.

The tail leg can be hydraulically retracted and extended, but the G2 did not make use of this system. The tail leg is an oil- and air-filled strut, which is fitted into the tail carrier section of the fuselage.

Fitted to the tail leg is a locking mechanism, which prevents shimmying on take-off and landing. A lever on the left-hand side of the cockpit operates this system, which must be in the OFF position for taxiing.

RIGHT: Tail-leg locking mechanism operating handle. Below is the cockpit vent door.
Matthew Starr

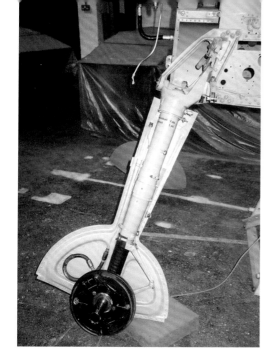

Brakes

The brake system consists of two servo-expanding brake units, operated by two hydraulic foot motors, mounted to the rear of the rudder pedals. The brakes can be operated individually by foot pressure on the rudder control pedals.

Flying controls

Ailerons, rudder, elevator, flaps and horizontal stabiliser make up the flying controls for the 109. The control column operates the ailerons

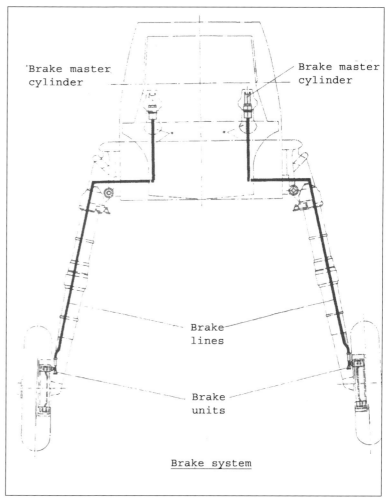

Brake system

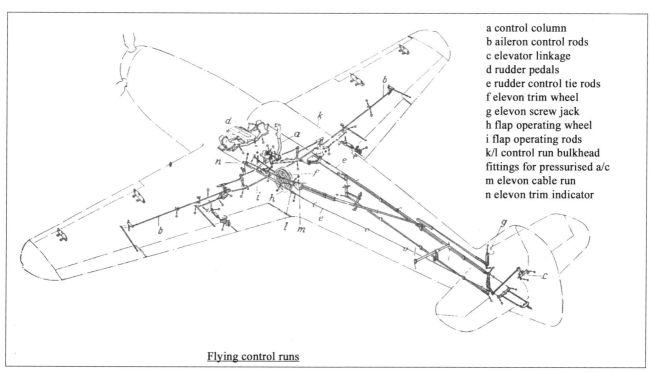

a control column
b aileron control rods
c elevator linkage
d rudder pedals
e rudder control tie rods
f elevon trim wheel
g elevon screw jack
h flap operating wheel
i flap operating rods
k/l control run bulkhead
fittings for pressurised a/c
m elevon cable run
n elevon trim indicator

Flying control runs

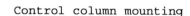

Control column mounting

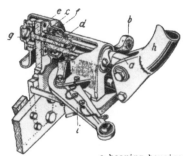

a control column shaft
b three arm lever
c oil seal
d bearing
e bearing housing
f circlip
g screwed joint
h control column
i elevon control lever

and the elevator, with the rudder being operated by pedals.

The horizontal stabiliser and the flaps are operated by hand wheels to the left of the pilot's seat, one wheel will lower and raise the flaps and the other will adjust the angle of the stabiliser.

Each aileron is constructed of a metal framework, covered with Irish linen, and attached to the wing at two hinge points. Connected to the aileron is a control lever, and then a series of control rods connects to the control column. Each aileron is mass balanced by a counter-weight, attached to its lower surface.

The rudder is also constructed of a metal framework, covered in Irish linen, and is attached to the fin unit and tail carrier using two

RIGHT: Rudder, elevator and landing flaps. *Matthew Starr*

hinges. Two tie rods, from the rudder pedals, are attached to a bell crank in the tail carrier, where two adjustable operating rods then connect to the lower rudder hinge. The rudder is also mass balanced using a cast weight in the tip fairing.

Elevators are constructed in the same way as the rudder and ailerons, and are attached by an outer hinge point and an inboard bearing and pin attachment pivot assembly and mass balanced using a cast weight located in the horn. A control rod from the pivot assembly attaches to a bell crank in the tail carrier assembly, where four tie rods, two top and two bottom, attach to a bell crank/balance weight assembly, on the right-hand side of the forward fuselage in the fuel tank bay area. From the forward bell crank, a series of control rods attach to the base of the control column.

The flaps are an all-metal construction and attach to the wing inboard of the ailerons and outboard of the cooler flaps using a piano hinge assembly, which runs the whole length of the flap. A control rod from each flap connects to a bell crank in the wing, from which another control rod connects to a screw jack under the cockpit floor. A series of chains and sprockets connect from this screw jack to the hand wheel in the cockpit, and when the pilot raises or lowers the flaps he can see what position the flaps are in by looking at the painted stencil on the inboard port flap shroud. This stencil

indicates the range of movement in the flap in increments of ten degrees.

The horizontal stabiliser (tailplane) is of an all-metal, flush riveted, shell construction. Each shell half consists of a skin and a Z-section spar, with a riveted hinge strip at each leading edge. The halves are attached together with a hinge pin. The shells are then closed together and riveted together at the trailing edge. It is fitted to the tailplane carrier with one large pivot bolt. At the front of the stabiliser there is a screw jack for adjusting the angle of the stabiliser. From the screw jack, a chain is attached to cables, which run along the top of the inside fuselage, down to a chain attached to the inboard hand wheel via a sprocket. A

ABOVE: Flap indicator markings on the port flap assembly. *Matthew Starr*

BELOW LEFT: Flap screw jack assembly. *D(Luft)T.2109 G-2*

BELOW: The radiator flaps in the open position, where the radiator can be clearly seen. *Matthew Starr*

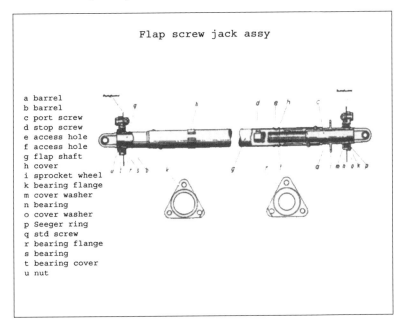

Flap screw jack assy

a barrel
b barrel
c port screw
d stop screw
e access hole
f access hole
g flap shaft
h cover
i sprocket wheel
k bearing flange
m cover washer
n bearing
o cover washer
p Seeger ring
q std screw
r bearing flange
s bearing
t bearing cover
u nut

Flying controls: range of movements

Ailerons	Up	22° 40'+/–1.5°
	Down	21° 40'+/–1.5°
Flaps	Down	40°+/–2°
Elevator up	33°+2° –1°	
Elevator down	34°+2° –1°	
Rudder left and right	34°+1° –2°	

When the hand wheel is operated the tailplane can move between +2° and –6°.

The leading edge slats are mounted to the port and starboard wings, in front of the leading edge, at ribs eight to thirteen. Each slat is fitted to two roller assemblies and slide bars at ribs nine and twelve. They are made from dural sheet, stiffened with solid ribs and a pinewood packing strip screws into the leading edge.

Armaments

The Bf109G-2 is fitted with two MG17 7.92mm machine guns, mounted on the top decking of the forward fuselage, which are fed by two ammunition boxes containing 500 rounds each, housed beneath the gun mounts in a space between the engine bulkhead and the gun support frame. These are operated electrically and by compressed air. The compressed air bottles are housed in the rear fuselage, under the battery tray. The guns are synchronised by two interrupter units, fitted to the engine forward of the magneto, which allow the guns to fire without hitting the propeller.

A 20mm cannon, MG151/20, is fitted at the rear of the engine on a mounting bracket fixed to the ancillary drive and when installed the breach of the cannon sits forward of the control column and between the pilot's legs. The cannon fires through a tube situated between the 'V' of the blocks in the crankcase

further chain, attached to the hand wheel via a sprocket, runs to the indicator unit, which is found on the lower left-hand side of the cockpit.

RIGHT: Horizontal stabiliser operating screwjack.
Black 6 Team

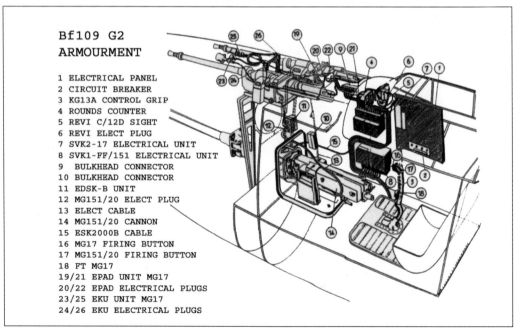

```
Bf109 G2
ARMOURMENT

 1 ELECTRICAL PANEL
 2 CIRCUIT BREAKER
 3 KG13A CONTROL GRIP
 4 ROUNDS COUNTER
 5 REVI C/12D SIGHT
 6 REVI ELECT PLUG
 7 SVK2-17 ELECTRICAL UNIT
 8 SVK1-FF/151 ELECTRICAL UNIT
 9 BULKHEAD CONNECTOR
10 BULKHEAD CONNECTOR
11 EDSK-B UNIT
12 MG151/20 ELECT PLUG
13 ELECT CABLE
14 MG151/20 CANNON
15 ESK2000B CABLE
16 MG17 FIRING BUTTON
17 MG151/20 FIRING BUTTON
18 FT MG17
19/21 EPAD UNIT MG17
20/22 EPAD ELECTRICAL PLUGS
23/25 EKU UNIT MG17
24/26 EKU ELECTRICAL PLUGS
```

RIGHT: Bf109G2 armament.
D(Luft)T.2109 G-2

ABOVE LEFT: MG17 installation with flash tubes and interrupter gear. *Matthew Starr*

ABOVE: MG17 mounting. *Matthew Starr*

LEFT: Rear fuselage battery tray and two compressed air bottles for the MG17 machine guns. *Matthew Starr*

BELOW LEFT: MG17 compressed air charging point. *Matthew Starr*

BELOW: Rear starboard engine compartment showing the MG17. Cold engine start pipe work is in yellow. The space under the top rear bearer attachment is for ammunition boxes for the MG17s. *Matthew Starr*

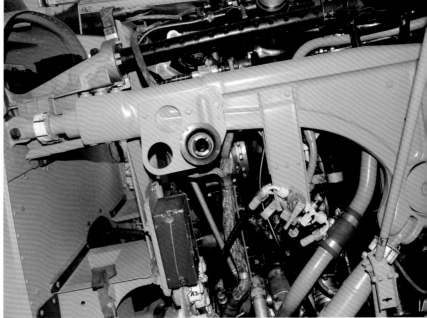

ABOVE: Removed DB605 engine. At the rear is the MG151 20mm cannon. *Black 6 Team*

FAR RIGHT: Control column with the MG151 firing button, which is guarded to avoid accidental discharge of the weapon. *Matthew Starr*

RIGHT: The Revi gunsight. *Matthew Starr*

RIGHT: K98 carbine stowed inside the rear fuselage. *Black 6 Team*

and is electrically operated. The 300 rounds of ammunition are fed from a bay in the port wing.

Both machine guns and cannon are fired with buttons on the control column stick top. The 20mm cannon button is guarded by a lever, which hinges forward to allow access to the button, and also becomes the firing trigger for the two machine guns.

Additional armament can be carried, as there is provision in each wing to mount a 20mm MG151/20, which would be housed in an external 'gondola'.

Cockpit and instrumentation

A three-part windscreen/canopy assembly, of tubular construction, covers the cockpit. The windscreen section is riveted to a metal fairing, secured to the forward fuselage. It consists of the front screen, a curved upper glazing and side windows. Behind the front screen there is 60mm thick armoured glass. In the upper corners of the windscreen section there are handgrips to aid entry to and exit from the cockpit.

The canopy section is split into two parts: the canopy and the rear canopy. The canopy opens to the right and is restrained by a cable attached to the rear canopy. This section has six perspex panels; the forward two slide open to allow fresh air ventilation. To the left of the canopy frame is the locking handle, which, when the canopy is shut, will lock it in place. For the protection of the pilot's head, at the rear of the canopy there is an armoured plate, 10mm thick with padding.

The rear canopy section is made up of three perspex panels and has an aerial mast mounted to it. In an emergency, the middle and rear sections can be jettisoned by pulling an emergency handle, which is situated to the upper left-hand side of the fuselage. By moving the handle, the restraining locating pins holding the rear section will be withdrawn and the rear canopy will jettison due to the release of two compressed springs, taking with it the canopy and thus allowing the pilot to safely bail out.

ABOVE: The three-part canopy and windscreen assembly. *Matthew Starr*

ABOVE: Canopy head armour and padding. *Matthew Starr*

LEFT: Aerial mast on the rear canopy. *Matthew Starr*

BELOW: Aerial porcelain fitting on the rear fuselage. This connects to the FuG7A radio inside the fuselage. *Matthew Starr*

BELOW: Rear aerial mount on fin unit. *Matthew Starr*

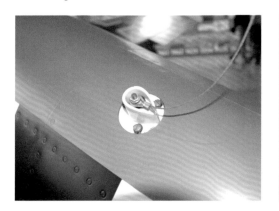

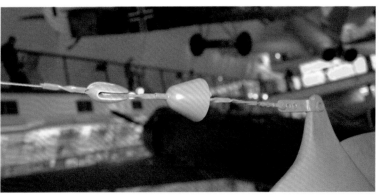

ABOVE: **Right-hand side of cockpit, showing electrical circuit breaker panel.** *Black 6 Team*

The pilot's seat consists of an adjustable seat pan and a seat back, which is fastened to the rear cockpit wall. It is made from an aluminium alloy. Shoulder straps are secured above this, and the lap straps are secured to the seat pan. Three sections of armour plate are fitted behind the rear cockpit wall to protect the pilot.

To the top rear section of the cockpit is a luggage compartment, which is only accessible when the canopy is opened. It is enclosed by a door and is a space large enough to hold a basic tool kit, the engine starting handle and emergency landing rations.

RIGHT: **Shoulder harness strap anchor points.** *Matthew Starr*

BELOW: **Luggage compartment with starter handle stowage.** *Matthew Starr*

Messerschmitt Bf109G-2, 'Black 6', cockpit

1. 60mm armour glass
2. P100 rounds counter indicator
3. Artificial horizon
4. Compass repeater
5. Altimeter
6. Air speed indicator
7. Power off button
8. Magneto switch
9. Plug cleaner handle
10. Starter switch below B4
11. Revi C/12D gunsight
12. Propeller pitch indicator
13. Oil/coolant temp gauge
14. RPM gauge
15. Fuel low-level warning light
16. Canopy release lever
17. U/c selector buttons
18. Windscreen wash lever
19. Emergency u/c lever
20. Fuel gauge
21. Fuel/oil pressure gauge
22./23. Cockpit lights
24. Tropical filter open/close handle
25./26. Rudder pedals with brake foot motors
27. Quick stop lever
28. U/c mechanical indicator
29. Throttle
30. Fuel cock lever
31. Throttle friction damper knob
32. Coolant shut-off valve handle
33. Priming tank
34. Horizontal stabiliser indicator
35. Horizontal stabiliser/flap operating wheels
36. MG151/20 button guard/MG17 trigger
37. MG151/20 firing button
38. Control column
39. MG151/20 cannon cover
40. Flying control lock
41. Seat pan
42. Pilot's harness lap straps
43. Coolant shut-off valve handle
44. Control handle for radiator flaps
45. Bomb release handle
46. Electrical circuit breaker panel
47. Oxygen regulator gauges
48. Radio/IFF control boxes
49. Oxygen regulator
50. Power on lever
51. Oxygen on/off valve

Matthew Starr

Instrument panel (left)

1. Air speed indicator
2. Artificial horizon
3. Altimeter
4. Compass
5. Power off button
6. Mag switch
7. Plug cleaner handle
8. U/c selector
9. U/c indicator
10. Guarded start switch
11. Canopy jettison lever
12. Cockpit light
13. Warning sign telling pilot to duck when operating canopy jettison lever
14. Cockpit air vent

Instrument panel (right)

1. Rounds counter box, not fitted
2. Rounds indicator
3. Rounds indicator
4. A/c clock
5. Gunsight electrical plug socket
6. Boost
7. Prop pitch indicator
8. Fuel low level warning
9. RPM gauge
10. Windscreen washer cock
11. Emergency u/c handle
12. Coolant/oil temperature gauge
13. Fuel contents gauge
14. Fuel/oil pressure gauge
15. Artificial horizon
16. Compass
17. Air speed indicator
18. Altimeter

LEFT: Cannon and machine gun rounds counter at the top of the instrument panel.
Matthew Starr

RIGHT:

1 Supercharger
2 Blanking plate for 20mm cannon
3 Hydraulic pump
4 Magneto
5 Electrical generator
6 Inertia starter (note – this is an electric starter, not a manual as should be fitted)
7 Fuel pump
8 Boost pressure control unit
9 Oil filter and ratchet cleaner
10 Free drive
11 Metering pump
12 Suppressor harness
13 Control valve links
14 Throttle lever links
15 Oil inlet
16 Oil drain plug
17 Air bleed connection
18 Control linkages

BELOW:

1 Prop shaft
2 Reduction gear
3 Engine bearer mounting
4 Interrupter gear location (not fitted)
5 Magneto
6 Inertia starter (note – this is an electric starter, not a manual as should be fitted)
7 Supercharger
8 Boost pipe
9 Boost pressure control unit
10 Plug lead harness
11 Camshaft cover

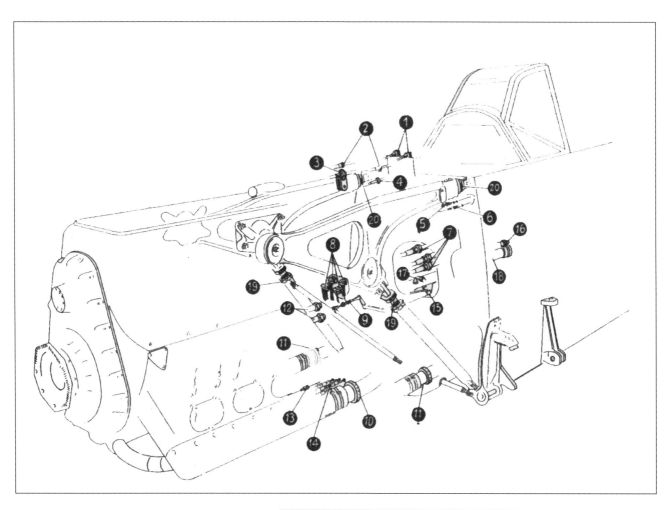

Engine

The engine fitted to the Bf109G-2 is the Daimler-Benz DB605A 35.7 litre V12, supercharged and fuel injected, weighing approximately 720kg (1,587lb). Major components of the engine are:

Crankcase

The crankcase is cast from aluminium alloy. Bolted to the front face is the reduction gear casing, with the accessory gearbox to the rear. The lower part of the casing forms two surfaces to which the cylinder blocks are fitted at an angle of 60° to each other.

ABOVE: Bf109 engine disconnection points. *D(Luft)T.2109 G-2*

LEFT: DB605 crankcase with the crankshaft removed. *Black 6 Team*

FAR LEFT: Daimler-Benz DB605A1 engine manufacturer's plate with Mercedes-Benz titling. *DB605 Parts Manual, 1942*

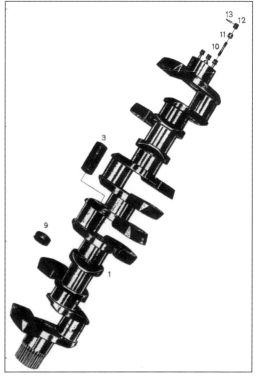

ABOVE: Crankshaft.
DB605 Parts Manual, 1942

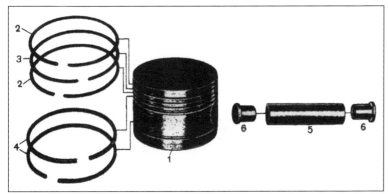

TOP: Inside the DB605: crankshaft connecting rods and in the middle is one of the geared cylinder nuts. *Black 6 Team*

ABOVE: Piston and rings. *DB605 Parts Manual, 1942*

RIGHT: DB605 with block removed showing pistons. Note the pistons are fitted with ring clamps. *Black 6 Team*

Crankshaft assembly

This six-throw crankshaft is machined from solid steel and at the front end it is splined to the pinion gear drive, while at the rear it has a flexible drive for the accessory gearbox. Twelve connecting rods, which act in pairs, are fitted to the crankshaft and pistons are fitted to these using floating gudgeon pins.

Cylinders

The two cylinder blocks each contain six threaded liners, which are bolted into each

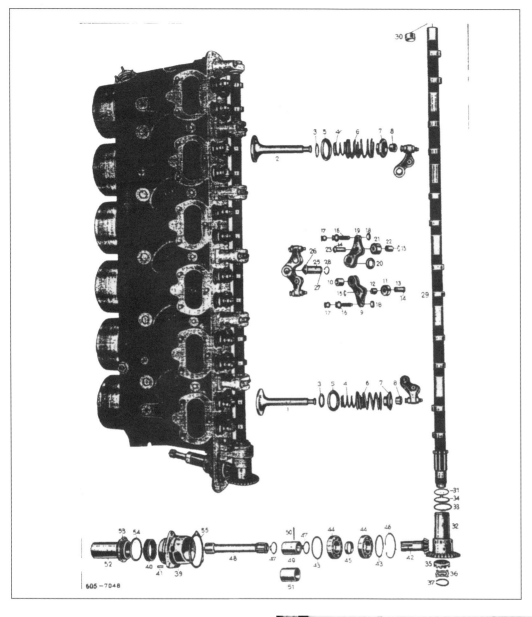

605-7048

block. Blocks are then tightened into the crankcase using cylindrical nuts.

Valve seats for two inlet and two exhaust valves are positioned in the base of each compression space. Suction and exhaust chambers are also accommodated within the cylinder block. Two spark plugs are screwed into the exhaust side of each cylinder and one injector nozzle is screwed in above each inlet. The camshaft for each block is enclosed by an oil tight cover, which, at the same time, acts as a collector sump for the oil that is returned to the oil tank by scavenge pumps fitted in the rear end of each cylinder cover.

Camshaft and valves

A camshaft, whose control cams actuate successively, via two short valve rockers, first the inlet and then the outlet valve, controls the valves of each row of cylinders. The valve rockers are pivoted at one end, while the axially adjusted ball cup is bolted to each of the other free ends containing a flattened ball. This ball on the valve shaft end, allowing adjustments to be made by the ball cup, supports the rocker arm.

Reduction gear and prop pitch control gear

The transmission of the engine power from the crankshaft to the propeller shaft is via a geared drive, the pinion of which is driven by the crankshaft via an intermediate gear wheel. The

TOP: DB605 engine with cam covers removed, exposing the camshafts and valves. In the centre is the fuel injection unit and forward of that is the propeller pitch motor. *Black 6 Team*

RIGHT: Reduction gear mechanism. *DB605 Parts Manual, 1942*

BELOW: Mercedes-Benz manufacturer's plate. *Black 6 Team*

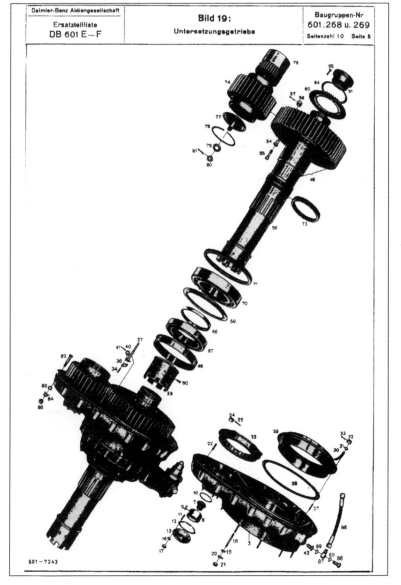

| Daimler-Benz Aktiengesellschaft | Bild 19: | Baugruppen-Nr |
| Ersatzteilliste DB 601 E—F | Untersetzungsgetriebe | 601.268 u. 269 Seitenzahl 10 Seite 5 |

601-7243

RIGHT: DB605 fitted and ready for dressing.
Black 6 Team

propeller pitch control gear is flanged on to the reduction gear casing.

Accessory drive

The gear wheels for the injection pump drive and accessory drives are located in the accessory gear case. This is bolted on to the rear wall of the crankcase. Fitted to this are: the twin magneto, the starter, fuel pump, coolant pump, oil pump and the supercharger. There is also provision to fit the following: generator, hydraulic pump and air compressor, if required, for pressurised aircraft.

Coolant pump

The coolant pump ensures the circulation of the coolant and is designed as a centrifugal pump with two outlet pipe connections, which are connected to the inlet connection of the cylinder blocks by means of flexible hoses. Coolant enters on the accessory side, bottom, into the cylinder blocks and flows into a pipe inside each block. Different sized holes are located at suitable positions in the pipe, through which the coolant is supplied at the required rate to the positions that are to be cooled, such as the path of the piston travel, the combustion chamber and the vicinity of the valve seats. The coolant then emerges from the front face of the right- and left-hand cylinder blocks, through a vapour separator, returning to the coolant pump via the radiators.

Oil pump

The pressure oil pump is a gear pump fitted in the housing of the coolant pump. The coolant pump shaft drives it by two spur gears. Bolted on to the casing of the pump is a filter. There are also two scavenge oil pumps fitted in the rear of each cylinder cover, they are double gear pumps that return oil through the oil cooler back to the tank. A pipe to the suction strainer also links the pump, which is located at the front end of the cylinder cover. This sucks away any oil collecting there during dive conditions.

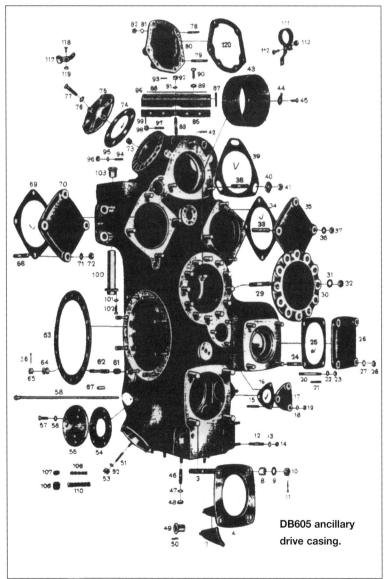

DB605 ancillary drive casing.

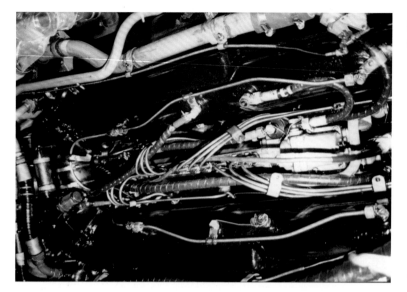

The fuel pump

This is a double gear pump, which is driven by the oil pressure pump via two spiral gears. A control piston regulates the fuel within the pump.

Fuel injection system

The fuel injection system consists of a 12-cylinder injection pump, mixture control, the fuel breather and the injection nozzle, screwed into the engine cylinders with the associated fuel pipes.

The task of the injection pump is to inject fuel at a specific rate, via the injection nozzles, into the cylinders. On the drive end of the injection pump is a device, in the cut-off housing, which allows the pilot, by pulling a lever in the cockpit, to interrupt the fuel into the cylinders, thereby shutting down the engine.

Supercharger

The supercharger serves to increase the charging of the cylinders in order to increase the power. This is necessary for flights at high altitude; otherwise the performance of the engine would decrease as a result of low air density. It operates automatically and continuously and consists mainly of a rotor in a casing. The rotor is driven by the accessory drive via an auxiliary shaft and a hydraulic coupling. Air to drive the supercharger is taken in via the prominent air intake on the left-hand side of the engine cowling.

Pressure oil, for the coupling, is delivered by a barometrically controlled metering pump, which maintains the boost pressure at all times.

Ignition system

The air fuel mixture is ignited by two spark plugs in each cylinder; the plugs are supplied with electrical current from a twin ignition magneto, fitted at the top of the accessory gearbox. The ignition coil in the twin magneto is energised through the aircraft electrical system by pulling a starter switch. A vibrator in the switch supplies the current, which is transformed into high voltage and is then supplied to the spark plugs.

DB605 supercharger assembly.

Cleaning the plugs can be carried out with the engine running by pulling a lever in the cockpit. This retards the ignition, allowing any oil or soot on the plugs to be burned off. The necessity for initiating this process is recognised by mag drop reading of over 50rpm. If the process does not improve the mag reading, there is another problem within the ignition system, which would need addressing.

Inertia starter

The starter motor, which is hand cranked by the starter handle on the right-hand side of the engine, causes the flywheel and its reduction gear to rotate. After winding for 20 seconds, the required speed of approximately 18,000rpm is reached. This high rpm is then reduced by planet gears and transmitted to the starter dog via a clutch housing. The pilot can then start the aircraft by pulling the start handle in the cockpit, which throws the starter dog into the back of the crankshaft, thus turning the engine over until it fires.

Engine controls

Control rods or cables from the cockpit operate all the engine controls and they either pass through the engine firewall bulkhead or through the cockpit floor to the engine itself.

Throttle

The throttle lever assembly is mounted on the left-hand side of the cockpit. The lever is operated using a linkage rod connected to a shaft forward of the cockpit front wall, where a second linkage rod, with a quick release coupling, connects to a lever on the engine.

Fuel cock

The fuel cock lever is situated in the throttle box and is connected to the fuel filter assemblies, under the cockpit floor, using a system of linkage rods. The fuel cock has four settings: OFF; P1, which operates one fuel filter cock; P2, which operates the second fuel filter cock; and P1/P2, which operates both.

Engine quick stop control

The engine quick stop control is cable-operated, mounted forward of the throttle control box. The cable passes under the

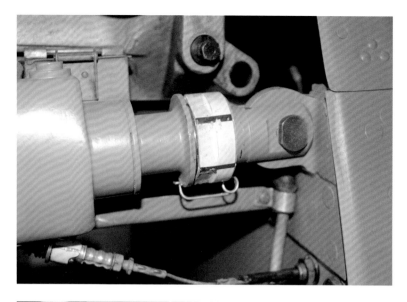

ABOVE: Port top rear engine bearer disconnection nut. *Matthew Starr*

LEFT: Throttle – yellow. Fuel cock lever – red. *Matthew Starr*

BELOW: Throttle linkage. *Matthew Starr*

RIGHT: Throttle lever
(middle), priming tank
(lower), and fuel cut-
off lever (forward) are
all painted yellow.
Matthew Starr

fuselage to the injection pump under the engine. Pulling the lever rearwards stops the engine.

Spark plug cleaner

Th spark plug cleaner is cable-operated and is mounted on the left-hand side of the instrument panel. The cable leads through the fuselage and is connected to the spark ignition lever mounted on the rear of the engine. During engine runs, if the mag drop is high, the pilot can pull the handle, which retards the ignition, which in turn cleans the spark plugs. On releasing the handle the engine returns to normal running and, hopefully, the mag drop will return to a normal reading.

Engine start controls

The engine start is a cable-operated gated handle, which is located on the left-hand side of the instrument panel and connects to a lever mounted on the port engine bearer. The lever is then connected by linkage rod to the starter motor. On engine start, once the winding of the starter motor is complete, the handle is pulled; it engages the starter to the starter dog at the back of the crankshaft and so turns the engine.

Coolant cooler flap control

This handle is situated on the right-hand side of the cockpit and operates a rotary valve

within the coolant system. This handle can be operated in ON, OFF or AUTOMATIC settings. ON opens the cooler flaps, OFF closes them and AUTO controls them so that they open and close as temperatures fluctuate.

Coolant cooler shut-off control

These are cable-operated controls situated to the left and right in the cockpit below the instrument panel. The cables then pass to two isolating valves on the delivery and return line of each port and starboard radiator system. They were only used in the event of damage by enemy action to the coolant system. Pulling the handle, on either side, isolates each individual system.

ABOVE: Left-hand side of the cockpit. The red knob is the canopy jettison lever; the warning sign above reads, translated: 'duck your head when operating the lever!'. *Matthew Starr*

LEFT: Oxygen regulator and gauges; bomb release handle in red; radiator cooler flap control handle above. *Matthew Starr*

Sand filter control

This is a cable-operated handle located to the left, under the instrument panel, and is used to open and close the sand filter as required.

Auxiliary fuel tank venting control

This handle is mounted on the left-hand wall of the cockpit and is connected to a valve forward of the cockpit front wall. Operating the handle allows fuel from the drop tank to access the engine via the main fuel tank.

Priming tank control

A small priming tank is located on the left-hand side of the cockpit, besides the pilot's seat. Before engine start a hand pump is pumped several times, which sprays vaporised fuel into each cylinder.

Non-destructive testing

Four methods of non-destructive testing (NDT) are available: an X-ray check, ultrasound, magnetic particle check and dye penetrant test.

X-ray tests are used to examine parts of the Messerschmitt that cannot be easily accessed, such as the wing spars. This check will usually show up any internal corrosion or cracking.

An ultrasound check uses sound waves to check cracking around the bore of a hole. A probe is inserted into the hole, for example the fin attachment holes, and a meter read-out indicates if there is any damage in the vicinity of the hole.

A magnetic particle test is used to check for cracks in ferrous metal components, such as the undercarriage mounting brackets. The component is painted with a fluid containing iron filings and an electric current is then passed through it, the sample will then be examined under an ultra-violet light that highlights any faults.

A dye penetrant test is used for checking for cracks in ferrous and non-ferrous metal components. The component is painted with fluorescent purple dye, then cleaned and sprayed with a white developer, which, after approximately 40 minutes, will highlight any cracks in purple.

Tools and specialist equipment

For day-to-day working on your project, a tool kit should include a good selection of metric spanners, sockets, screwdrivers, files, locking wire pliers and snips, as found in a basic kit.

For more specialised jobs, such as tightening the ring nuts on the engine blocks, a pair of reversible torque wrenches is required. Other speciality tools, such as piston ring clamps, a bearing extractor kit and a propeller nut socket. are essential.

Larger equipment, such as an aircraft lifting beam and tail and wing trestles, will be invaluable. Ballast weights complete with a strop, to stop the tail from lifting when jacked, will also be necessary.

Also consider a roll over frame, which will allow you to work on your engine when it is removed from the frame, and an engine lifting beam for ease of removal.

Servicing the Bf109

The servicing guidelines below are taken from an original wartime manual (D Luft T.2109G-2), adapted by the Black 6 team and approved for use with Black 6 by the CAA. Individual owners will follow a similarly approved schedule.

Pre-flight checks
1. Make sure the fuel tank is full.
2. Check the engine oil level is correct.
3. Check the coolant system is full.
4. Check the hydraulic tank is to the correct level.
5. Fill the engine start priming tank with fuel.
6. Check tyre pressures – 4.5atus.
7. Check fuel, oil, coolant pipes and unions for leaks.
8. Check flying controls for damage, freedom and range of movement.
9. Check that the electrical fuel pump is operating, by listening to it.
10. Make sure all cowlings and panels are secured and locked.
11. Clean the windscreen and canopy.
12. Examine the fuselage and wing skins for distortion and cracks.
13. Check oil cooler and radiators are clear of debris and the matrix is not showing signs of leakage.

After-flight checks
The after-flight checks are the same as the pre-flight, however, instead of checking levels you would be refilling the tanks. Coolant and oil can only be topped up after cooling down, and the aircraft would be cleaned.

12½-hour flying time service
1. Inspect and clean the fuel and oil filters.
2. Grease the coolant pump.
3. Clean the hydraulic filter.
4. Carry out compression test.
5. Check oleo strut pressure.
6. Check the cylinder locking nuts for tightness.
7. Examine and lubricate flying control bearings and linkages.
8. Examine and lubricate all engine control linkages.
9. Complete all pre-flight checks as listed above.

25-hour servicing (annual)
1. Remove all access panels and inspect the airframe internally.
2. Check cable tensions on horizontal stabiliser.
3. Check elevator and rudder tie rod tensions.
4. Carry out engine oil change.
5. Remove spark plugs, clean and test.
6. Check the bolts on the supercharger casing for tightness.
7. Check the attachment bolts on the fuel injection mounting for cracks.
8. Inspect the injection pipes.
9. Carry out undercarriage retraction tests.
10. Carry out the maintenance for the 12½-hour servicing.

200-hour engine check
Engine is removed for overhaul.

Appendix 1

Airworthy Bf109s and Buchóns

At the time of writing, in early 2009, there were five airworthy or potentially airworthy Bf109s and seven airworthy Hispano Buchóns at different locations worldwide. This was in addition to the approximately 61 Bf109s and 28 Hispano Buchóns, plus three Avia-built aircraft, that exist in museums or in private collections as non-flying exhibits. Of course, it must be stressed that this number can go up or down, as several potentially airworthy museum exhibits or privately-owned examples were allegedly on the long road to being made airworthy at that time, while two of the genuinely airworthy aircraft belonging to EADS/Messerschmitt Foundation in Germany were actually under rebuild having suffered non-fatal accidents during 2008.

Messerschmitt Bf109

Bf109E-3 WNr 1342 (N342FH), ex-6/JG 51 'Yellow 8' (Pilot: Eduard Hemmerling) – crashed 29 July 1940. **'Yellow 8'**, Flying Heritage Collection, Everett, Washington State, US. This aircraft is part of the collection of Paul Allen of Microsoft fame.

Bf109E-4 (E-1) WNr 3579 (CF-EML), ex-LG 2 'White 14', ex-Bf 109E-7 4/JG 5 'White 7' – crashed 2 August 1942. **'White 14'**, Russell Aviation Group, Ontario, Canada.

Bf109G-6 WNr 163306, ex-RQ+DR, ex-JGr.

LEFT TOP: A number of Hispano Buchóns have been converted into Bf109 look-alikes for museum display. One of the most convincing is this example in the Luftwaffenmuseum at the former RAF Gatow airfield on the outskirts of Berlin. It is painted as a Bf109G-2, 'Yellow 4', in North Africa campaign markings. *Malcolm V. Lowe*

LEFT: Bf109E-4 owned by the Russell Aviation Group in Canada. *Jerry Day*

West 'Red 3' – crashed 28 May 1944, **'Red 3'**, Fundacja Polskie Orly, Warsaw, Poland.
Bf109G-10 WNr unknown (D-FDME), **'Black 2 + -'**, ex-Hans Dittes, EADS/Messerschmitt Foundation, Manching, Germany. *Note*: some components from Bf109G-10 WNr 151591 used in restoration, and wings from an HA-1112-M1L (possibly C.4K-40). Damaged in landing accident at Berlin Air Show ILA 2008 in May 2008 but under rebuild.
Bf109G-14 WNr 610937 (N109EV), ex-Bf109G-10/U-4, ex-Bulgarian air force, ex-Yugoslavian

ABOVE: Looking very authentic, this is the airworthy Bf109G-10/ Buchón composite, D-FDME, Black 2. At the time of writing it was still under repair following its landing accident in May 2008. *Messe-Berlin*

LEFT: One of the earliest-surviving complete Bf109s is this early Bf109E, Werk Nummer 790, which is on display at the Deutsches Museum in Munich, southern Germany. A Bf109E-1/E-3, it is painted as a Bf109E-4, Werk Nummer 2804. *Malcolm V. Lowe*

RIGHT: The Czechoslovakian-designed, Junkers Jumo 211-engined derivatives of the Bf109 are now very rare, with only three non-airworthy survivors known to exist. Two are displayed at the Letecké Muzeum (Aviation Museum) at Prague-Kbely in the Czech Republic, a two-seat CS-199 and this single-seat S-199. The very different nose of the aircraft, which was redesigned to take the bulky Jumo 211, is evident in this view of the single-seat S-199 c/n 178. *Malcolm V. Lowe*

BELOW: There are various Spanish-built Hispano Buchóns displayed in museums, including this non-airworthy HA-1112-M1L C.4K-156 in Spanish Air Force colours, at the Musée de l'Air et de l'Espace, Le Bourget, Paris. *Graham Young*

air force (s/n 9664), now **'Green <<'**, Evergreen Ventures (EAM), McMinnville, Oregon, US.

Hispano Buchón

HA-1112-M1L c/n 67 C.4K-31 (G-AWHE/ N109ME), appeared in *Battle of Britain* film, 'Red 8', now **'Yellow 14',** registered to Magnificent Obsessions Ltd, Louth, UK.
HA-1112-M1L c/n 139 C.4K-75 (D-FWME), appeared in *Battle of Britain* film, 'Yellow 11', now **'Red 7 + ~'**, EADS/Messerschmitt Foundation, Manching, Germany. *Note*: powered by DB605 engine. Damaged in landing accident in Germany in April 2008 but was later repaired.
HA-1112-M1L c/n 156 C.4K-87 (D-FMBB), now **'FM+BB'**, EADS/Messerschmitt Foundation, Manching, Germany. *Note*: powered by DB605 engine.
HA-1112-M1L c/n 172 C.4K-102 (G-BWUE), appeared in *Battle of Britain* film, 'Red 7', now **'Red 1'**, Spitfire Ltd, based at Duxford, UK.
HA-1112-M1L c/n 201 C.4K-131 (OO-MAF), appeared in *Battle of Britain* film, ex-Victory Air Museum, now **'White 1'**, Eric Vormezeele Collection, Brasschaat, Belgium.
HA-1112-M1L c/n 234 C.4K-169 (N109W), appeared in *Battle of Britain* film, 'Red 5', now **'<<- + -'**, Harold Kindsvater, Castle Air Force Base, California, US.
HA-1112-M1L c/n 235 C.4K-172 (N109GU), appeared in 'Battle of Britain' film, ex-Victory Air Museum, now **'<- + -'**, Cavanaugh Flight Museum, Addison, Texas, US.

Appendix 2

Glossary and Translations

AG   Aktiengesellschaft (roughly equivalent to a joint-stock company)

AGO   various names seem to have made up this abbreviation, including Aerowerke Gustav Otto

ANR   Aeronautica Nazionale Repubblicana (Italy)

ATG   Allgemeine Transportanlage GmbH (sometimes written as Allgemeine Transportanlage Gesellschaft mbH)

Bf   abbreviation for Messerschmitt aircraft; generally the Bf109 series was the last from this manufacturer to use this abbreviation, the company changing its name from BFW to Messerschmitt and so subsequently using 'Me'

BFW   Bayerische Flugzeugwerke AG, the original designer of the Bf109 and other types such as the Bf110

BMW   Bayerische Motorenwerke AG (sometimes also written Bayerische Motoren Werke AG)

cg   centre of gravity

c/n   construction number

CFE   Central Fighter Establishment (RAF)

DB   Daimler-Benz

Dipl-Ing   Diplom-Ingenieur (literally a Diploma Engineer, roughly equivalent to an engineering degree in a specific engineering subject)

DLH   Deutsche Lufthansa

EADS   the European Aeronautic, Defence and Space Company

FOD   foreign object damage

FuG   Funk Gerät (literally radio set or apparatus, the generic designation used for radio, IFF, etc., equipment in the Bf109, Fw190, Ta152 and other types)

Fw   Focke-Wulf Flugzeugbau GmbH

Geschwaderstab   fighter wing headquarters

GmbH   Gesellschaft mit beschränkter Haftung (roughly equivalent to a British Limited Company)

GM   abbreviated designation for the GM 1 nitrous oxide used for boosting the power output of some German piston engines

Höhenjäger   high-altitude fighter

hp   horse power

IFF   Identification Friend/Foe

IWM   Imperial War Museum

Jagdstaffel   fighter squadron

JG   Jagdgeschwader (Luftwaffe fighter wing)

LG   Landing Ground

Ltd   Limited Company (UK)

MBB   Messerschmitt-Bölkow-Blohm

Me   abbreviation for Messerschmitt aircraft; generally the Bf109 series was one of the last from this manufacturer to use this abbreviation, the company changing its name from BFW to Messerschmitt and so subsequently using 'Me' for types such as Me209, Me410, etc.

MMW   Mitteldeutsche Metallwerke GmbH, Erfurt (Mimetall)

MW   abbreviated designation for the MW 50 methanol-water used for boosting the power output of some German piston engines

MU   Maintenance Unit (RAF)

NASM   National Air and Space Museum (United States)

OKL   Oberkommando der Luftwaffe (Luftwaffe High Command)

R   Rüstsatz (plural, Rüstsätze), the conversion kits or sets (often concerned with add-on armament options) for installation in the field

RAAF   Royal Australian Air Force

RAF   Royal Air Force

Reichsverteidigung   Reich defence fighter force

Revi   Reflexvisier (literally reflex gunsight, the generic designation for gunsights carried in some German military aircraft)

RLM   Reichsluftfahrtministerium, the Third Reich's aviation ministry

RM   Reichsmark (the unit of currency of the Third Reich)

rpg   rounds per gun

rpm   revolutions per minute

s/n   serial number

Stab   headquarters

Ta   abbreviation for the name of Dipl.-Ing. Kurt Tank, the talented designer and technical director of the Focke-Wulf company

TA   Technisches Amt, the RLM's technical designs organisation

U   Umrüst-Bausatz (plural, Umrüst-Bausätze), the conversion kits or sets installed at the factory to give a particular equipment fit or capability

UK   United Kingdom

US   United States

V   Versuchs or Versuchsmuster, the term used to describe an experimental or test airframe, not necessarily a prototype

VDM   Vereinigte Deutsche Metallwerke AG, propeller manufacturer

VHF   Very High Frequency (radio)

WNr   Werk Nummer (German construction number)

Appendix 3

Imperial and metric equivalents of weapons calibres and weights

Metric	Imperial	Metric	Imperial
7.7mm	0.303in	21cm	8.27in
7.92mm	0.312in		
13mm	0.512in	50kg	110lb
15mm	0.59in	250kg	551lb
20mm	0.787in	500kg	1,102lb
30mm	1.181in	300 litres	66 UK gallons

Appendix 4

Useful contacts

Airframe Assemblies
Steve Vizard
Hangar 6S, Isle of Wight Airport, Sandown, Isle of Wight PO36 OJP
Produces replacement airframes.

Anglia Radiators
Unit 4, Stanley Road, Cambridge CB5 8LB
Builds and repairs radiators and oil coolers.

ARCO
Duxford Airfield, Cambridge CB2 4QR
Provides maintenance facilities for historic aircraft.

Argus Fluidtechnik GmbH
Pforzheimer Strasse 126, 76275 Ettlingen, Germany
Oil and fuel hoses, and end fittings.

Charleston Aviation
109 Workshop, Great Horkesley, Colchester, Essex
Restores 109 Emils to flying condition.

Dunlop Tyres
40 Fort Parkway, Erdington, Birmingham B24 9HL
Supplier of tyres.

Hanley Smith
7 South Road, Templefields, Harlow, Essex CM20 2AP
Overhauls undercarriage components.

Hoffmann Propeller GmbH & Co. KG
Kuepferlingstr. 9, D-83022 Rosenheim, Germany
Manufacture of wooden propeller blades and overhaul of propeller hubs.

Premier Fuel Systems Ltd
Willow Industrial Park, Trent Lane, Castle Donington, Derby DE74 2NP
Manufacturer of composite rubber fuel tanks.

Skycraft
12 Silver Street, Litlington, Royston, Hertfordshire SG8 0QE
Builds and refurbishes propellers.

Supermarine Aero Engineering Ltd
Mitchell Works, Steventon Place, Burslem, Stoke-on-Trent, Staffordshire ST6 4AS
Machine components.

Vintage Fabrics
Mitchell Hangar, Audley End Airfield, Saffron Waldon, Essex CB11 4LH
Fabric for flying control surfaces, and aircraft spraying and artwork.

Index